The Formula for
Selling Alarm Systems

THE FORMULA FOR SELLING ALARM SYSTEMS

Lou Sepulveda, C.P.P.

Butterworth-Heinemann

Boston   Oxford   Johannesburg   Melbourne   New Delhi   Singapore

Recognizing the importance of preserving what has been written,
Butterworth–Heinemann prints its books on acid-free paper
whenever possible.

Library of Congress Cataloging-in-Publication Data
Sepulveda, Lou.
    The formula for selling alarm systems / by Lou Sepulveda.
        p.   cm.
    Includes index.
    ISBN 0-7506-9752-0 (pbk.)
    1. Selling—Electronic alarm systems. 2. Selling. I. Title.
HF5439.S39S47   1997
621.389′28′0688—dc20   96-26664
                                                        CIP

British Library Cataloguing-in-Publication Data
A catalogue record for this book is available from the British Library.

The publisher offers special discounts on bulk orders of this book.
For information, please contact:

Manager of Special Sales
Butterworth–Heinemann
313 Washington Street
Newton, MA 02158–1626
Tel: 617-928-2500
Fax: 617-928-2620

For information on all Security publications available, contact our
World Wide Web home page at: http://www.bh.com/bh/

10 9 8 7 6 5 4 3 2 1

Printed in the United States of America

Contents

Preface

Over the past twenty-eight years, I have been fortunate to be in the greatest business of all—the sales business. During those years I have read dozens of books and attended numerous seminars on the subject of selling. All were good in their own way, and I can honestly say I learned something each time. However, something was missing.

The purpose of this book is to clear up some of the mysteries of selling; to share some of the ideas that have been shared with me, and to provide the reader with a road map—a step-by-step method of selling and closing.

At my sales training clinics, novice and experienced salespeople confide their frustrations to me. They want to improve their selling skills but don't know how. Most have had little to no sales training and have learned, at best, from books they've read or from audio and video tapes they've listened to or watched. Each left them short.

Ten, fifteen, and even twenty year sales veterans have confessed their lack of solid knowledge of sales structure. My seminars and now this book have been designed to provide the needed structure, to end the mystery, to expose the magic, to uncover the secrets of successful selling.

This book was specifically designed to help you sell products directly to the consumer, but if your responsibility is to sell anything to anybody, the information in this book will be your guide. I suggest you read it twice or more and then refer to specific chapters as a reference as situations arise.

I encourage you to apply the principles and steps in the book for a minimum of twenty-one days; it takes twenty-one days to form a habit. After this time you will be more successful selling—I guarantee it.

What is selling? Selling is the process of causing someone (the prospect) to think as you do. For example, if I sell airplanes and you are my prospect, my task is to cause you to think as I do. If I think my airplane is the best airplane for you and I am successful in causing you to think as I do, then you will believe my airplane is the best for you and will want to own it. If I believe that the price I'm asking for the airplane is a bargain, none better, and I am successful in causing you to think as I do, then you, too, will believe the plane is a bargain and will want to buy it. If I think the time to buy is right now, today, and I am successful in causing you to believe as I do, then you will want to have it now, if you believe as I do. If I believe and think my company is the best company for your needs, then you too will think my company is the best company from which to buy, and so you will.

Your task throughout your sales career is to cause your prospect to think as you do. As long as your thinking is not stinking, you'll be successful.

The Formula for Selling Alarm Systems

1

From One to Ten

I was once told by a sales guru that you can measure the entire human race on a scale of one to ten, one being the easiest person to sell and ten the hardest. There are people who will buy anything from anybody who tries to sell it to them, and there are those who wouldn't buy a genuine one thousand dollar bill from a salesperson for one dollar. The rest of the human race falls somewhere between the two extremes. On the basis of that, the guru said, even the weakest of salespeople can make a sale, if they make enough calls and ask enough people to buy what they have to sell.

That bit of wisdom was shared with me when I began my career in sales. To me at the time, it was a comforting piece of reality. Now, more than twenty-eight years later, I find nothing has changed. That reality still exists and still provides the young people I train with comfort in their chosen career of selling.

On the pages to follow, I explain why this reality is so and how to take full advantage of it. I put facts in perspective and develop a bit of structure for you to follow. In that way you'll have a road map to a successful selling career. First let me take you back to when my sales career started.

In 1964 I received an honorable discharge from the navy. After a short career in a rock and roll band, I went out looking for my first real civilian job. At that time a good income for a non-college graduate was between $400 and $450 per month. You could purchase a new car for $1,500. My goal was to find a job that would pay $450, which was an ambitious goal ($450 per month in 1964 is equivalent to $4,000 per month today.)

If you think back to when you first looked for a job, you may have faced the same problem I did. Every place I applied said I needed experience. Whereupon I would ask, "How can I get experience if you won't give me a job?" And so it would go. Does this sound familiar? The days and weeks went by, and I became more and more frustrated and desperate. Then one day as I scanned the help wanted ads, I noticed an ad that read as follows:

> Men wanted to move stock from warehouse. $550 per month guaranteed, no experience necessary. Apply at 235 Claiborne Court.

I couldn't believe my eyes. The ad said "no experience necessary." It also said $550 per month. $550 per month to move stock from a warehouse! That had to be the best forklift job I ever heard of. Even if I had to carry the stock on my back or head for the $550, this was surely a tremendous opportunity.

I was the first one waiting at the Claiborne Court address when it opened the next morning. In fact, I was there before the sun came up. When the office opened, a secretary handed me an application and a test and directed me to a conference room, set up classroom style, to complete the application and test. As I started filling out the paper work, more applicants arrived. Before I finished, at least thirty-five people were in the room. I remember thinking, "Oh no!, they can't have thirty-five openings. This competition is going to be fierce."

Without completely realizing it, I began sizing up the other applicants, measuring them against myself. Some were younger, right out of high school. I remember thinking, "They're too young. Surely the company would prefer to hire someone like me who has already completed his military service and is more mature." Others were older than I, and I found reasons they should hire me over them.

I continued to the second form given to me, the test. I noticed that it was different from any other I had taken. The test focused on attitudes instead of fact. For instance, I recall that one question was as follows:

> If you are standing in line to get into a theater, and someone walks up and cuts in front of the line or somewhere in front of you, would you
>
> A.   Say nothing
> B.   Tell the person to go to the back of the line
> C.   Get in front of the person who cut
> D.   Complain to the theater management

The test was full of psychological and attitude questions. However, I was more concerned with the 35 people in the room than I was with the strangeness of the test, so I continued.

After we were finished, a well-dressed man, apparently the manager, entered the room. He introduced himself and welcomed us. He apologized for the number of people in the room, but he explained that the opportunity was so great, it was no real surprise to him so many people attended. I had to agree with him. After all, we were talking about $550 per month! All I wanted was $450. With $550 I'd practically be rich!

The company executive went on to explain that everyone in the room wouldn't qualify for the job. "Only the cream comes to the top," he said, and that is what he was looking for—the best of the best.

The executive further stated that not all people are destined for greatness. Some people fail in life and are relegated to the menial positions and jobs. Some aspire to and achieve greatness. Others do not feel qualified, have low self-esteem, and seek and achieve in the more menial, low-paying careers. And that's okay, he said. Someone has to do it. Someone has to pick up our garbage. Someone has to clean the street and work in the sewer. God bless them. "However," he emphasized, "I don't want that someone to be me. What about you?" he asked. "Will you aspire to and achieve greatness or will you clean our streets?"

As the executive talked, I grew taller in my chair. I thought, "I will be among the great. I won't be relegated to street cleaning. You won't find this guy in the sewer."

After a few more challenging words, the company executive broke the meeting for coffee and restroom time. He did say, however, that when we returned in approximately 15 minutes, the room would have fewer people. "There won't be 35 people here. Some of you already know your destiny in life. Although the opportunity is at hand to change destiny, some of you will accept your fate and will be the street cleaners of the world." And to them he said, "Thank you and God bless. It is hard and dirty work, but someone has to do it. And I want to take this opportunity to thank you now."

Fifteen minutes later, the meeting restarted. As the executive predicted, there were fewer people than before. Eight to ten had disappeared, and I was glad. The odds were getting better. My chances of getting this job had improved.

The company executive began part two of his meeting by telling us the history of his company. It was a national company and apparently quite successful. The executive began to ask us questions. He asked how many hours per day would be fair for his company to expect us to work? Some answered eight; others, to my surprise, answered six; others, including me, answered ten to twelve. The executive then asked how many days per week we should work? Some answered five, others four, and others, including me, said six. As we answered the questions, the executive wrote our answers on the blackboard behind him. He explained that the company manufactured a product called a home sanitronic system. He opened a box and began to demonstrate the most wonderful product I had ever seen. I wasn't sure exactly what it was. However, it did everything.

I remember the executive asking us how much we thought it cost to pay for an exterminating service to spray for roaches. I know that New Orleans had big roaches and lots of them, but I didn't know how much exterminating services cost. When he said that it cost an average of $25.00 per month, that sounded reasonable to me. Next the executive showed how this system, with just pennies worth of a chemical crystal, would fog a home in a way that most exterminators could not. The fog would get into cracks and crevices where roaches hide. The executive said one could accomplish all this for only pennies a month, saving more than $20 each month.

If that weren't enough, the executive went on to demonstrate how one could remove one attachment and connect another. The same machine then could polish silver and a car using simonizing wax, which was hard to work with but was inexpensive. With this system, the application and buffing process were extremely fast and easy. The executive asked how much we thought a good car waxer and buffer should cost. We all guessed different but close prices.

The executive then asked what we considered the dirtiest part of our houses. Some answered the garage, others behind the appliances in the kitchen and various other locations throughout the home. The executive told us that the dirtiest part of the house was the bed we slept on. He wanted to know if we all awoke every morning with a bad taste in our mouths, kind of pasty? "Do you awake with morning breath," he asked? Sure, we answered.

The executive opened a book and read a quote from a Kansas City laboratory stating that humans shed skin. While we sleep, we toss, turn, and roll around in our bed, shedding skin the whole time. This skin grinds into the sheet and then into the mattress. In fact, the Kansas City laboratory said, if you have owned your mattress more than three years, you have shed sufficient skin, and ground enough of this fine, gray skin powder in your mattress, to form another person. "Did you know you were sleeping with another person?" the executive asked. Yuck! This was a chilling thought.

The laboratory report went on to explain how colds and germs spread through this body ash. The good news was that this amazing system the company produced also eliminated this disgusting body ash. Boy, was I impressed! I would buy this system if I had the money. The demonstration went on for about an hour. As the executive explained the features, we discovered the machine was also a vacuum cleaner, a floor waxer, a carpet shampoo cleaner, a buffer, an exterminator, and a polisher. The product did everything but cook dinner.

At this point the company executive announced another short break. He explained once again that some people who had not left earlier would now leave. And it was okay with him. After all, he only wanted the real achievers to stick around to learn more. That was okay with me also.

When we returned there were fewer of us in attendance. The company executive explained how we would move stock from the warehouse. We would do so by showing this wonderful product to people, and when they bought it, we would have effectively moved the product from the warehouse. It was, of course, a sales job we were talking about, one that paid handsomely to the individual who believed in and who applied the fundamentals of sales.

The reason I tell this story, almost verbatim, is that what happened that day changed my life. Kirby, the vacuum cleaner company, introduced me to sales. I would not have answered the ad had they advertised for a sales trainee. I didn't consider myself a sales type. However, because they "tricked" me into listening to their story, I became a top sales producer and later a sales manager and trainer. Selling has been great to me. I will always owe a debt of gratitude to Kirby for providing the initial shove and the follow-up training that has helped shape my career.

By the way, the person who first told me about the one out of ten who will buy anything and the one out of ten who will buy nothing was Roy Bell. He was the owner of the New Orleans Kirby franchise that hired me in 1964. Also noteworthy is that Kirby lied when they said I could earn $550 per month. I worked for them while attending college and never made $550 per month. From the very first month I always made more. Sometimes to my delight, I made a whole lot more.

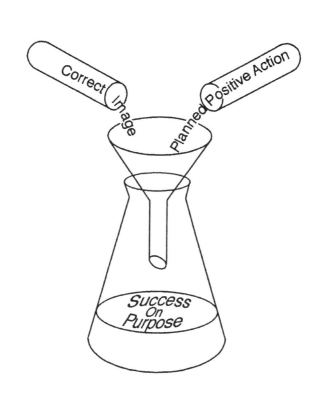

2

The Formula for Sales

CI + PPA = SOP

Correct Image + Planned Positive Action = Success on Purpose

During my years in sales, I have come to the conclusion that salespeople are only as good as their self-image allows them to be. If your self-image says you are good at what you do, you are or will be. Conversely, if your self-image is that of a failure, fail you will. Like it or not, this is the way it is. Your brain is a computer that produces what it's been programmed to produce. Program success, and success it delivers. Program failure, and the result is automatic.

We were all born with our very own "personal" computer, our brain. It is greater than all the computers in existence today. The output of our personal computer is controlled directly by what we think, what we believe, and, all to often, what other people tell us to think and believe. In short we are capable of doing almost anything we set our mind to do, depending on the programming we feed it. Almost anything is possible, as long as we believe strongly enough. "Faith (belief) can move mountains."

Numerous books have been written on the subject of the power of our minds. *Think and Grow Rich*, *The Power of Positive Thinking*, and *Psycho-Cybernetics* are just a few. However, *Pyscho-Cybernetics*, by Maxwell Maltz, best explains how your brain functions and how you can and do program it. The result, your self-image, is a direct result of your conscious belief in your ability to perform a task. Change the belief and the results will change.

Correct image, in the formula of selling, also has to do with how people see you. The image you portray is how prospects perceive you. Study of the brain also suggests, however, that one cannot act in conflict with one's self-image. If your image of yourself is that of a failure, you will act as a failure and therefore be perceived as a failure. The output is out of your control. You must act in accord with the image you have of yourself. To change the output, the image you have of yourself and the image others have of you, you must change the input, the internal programming that serves as the foundation of your self-image.

So how do we accomplish this task of internal programming? How does one reverse the negative input stored within? You start by recognizing and believing in the power of your mind. Once you truly understand and believe that you are in control of your destiny, that you control your emotions and feelings, that you control the way people see you, you are on the way to change.

Don't let me mislead you. I'm not minimizing the enormity of the task I've just suggested to you. Professional psychologists make a living helping people sort out the emotional web of programming in their minds. Start with the fundamental belief in the power of your mind, identify the negative programming, and then begin reversing the programming. Enter positive programming. Find ways to improve the weakness that supports the negative program. Read. Study the area in which you're weak. You'll improve, if you believe you can.

Correct image often begins with the *external* you. How do you feel about yourself when you wear a new suit? How do you feel about yourself when you are neatly groomed, with a fresh haircut, nice clothing, and polished shoes. Contrast that feeling with how you feel about yourself when the opposite is true. When your hair is too long or unmanageable. When you are dirty and your clothes are old and messy and you're in need of a bath.

This may seem to be an unfair comparison, but I'm trying to make a point. As a salesperson, the better you look, the better you feel about yourself, the better people around you will feel about you. As a manager, I've always required salespeople who work for me to wear a suit, white or blue dress shirt, and a nice tie, and a nice dress or ladies business suit for saleswomen. I know the look I just described goes a long way toward improving one's image. I'm not saying there is anything wrong with a pair of casual slacks and a golf shirt. However, the suit looks nicer, more professional.

In my seminars salespeople in attendance have argued that the area of the country they work doesn't require a suit. They argue that a suit actually works against the salesperson. The prospect considers people who wear suits "slick," they argue. I disagree. You never have to apologize for being neatly groomed and in a business suit. Prospects who want you to be more casual usually say so. It's easy then to remove the jacket, remove the tie, and even roll up your sleeves. Now you look relaxed and casual. However, it's near impossible to dress up for an appointment when you've arrived in casual dress.

Have you ever gone to a party or function dressed casually and once there discovered everyone but you is dressed formally? It's an awful feeling. There is no place to hide. The only good thing to do is leave. The same is true when going on a sales appointment. Always dress up, you'll be dressed correctly ninety percent of the time.

Influences on Self-Image

- Clothing
- Personal hygiene
- Physical appearance
- Command of language
- Knowledge and competence
- Success

All the external influences on the list are things about which you can do something. Change the external you, and you'll be on your way to improving the internal you.

Internal influences affect your self-image and the image you portray to the prospect. However, internal influences aren't so easily changed. An internal influence can be the way you think, what you believe in, your personal integrity, honesty, and care and concern for others. All of these factors affect the manner in which you portray yourself to others.

The difference between *smooth* and *slick* comes to mind. Both can describe the salesperson who made the sale. However, the difference in how the prospect perceives the salesperson is enormous. I'd much rather be described as a smooth salesperson than a slick one. *Slick* connotes slippery, slimy, untrustworthy, unbelievable, all negatives.

Both the smooth and the slick salespeople may say identical things about a product or service. Both may use identical closing techniques. However, how you feel about the salesperson as a prospect and whether you would ever recommend the salesperson to a friend are at issue. The difference can often be rooted in the belief in what one is selling coupled with the belief that the prospect needs the product. The customer's need should be the driving force in the sale, not the salesperson's need for a commission. Integrity and honesty are paramount.

Speaking of integrity, I'm reminded of a story about a young boy who at school was part of a discussion of the word *integrity* and its meaning. After returning home that day the boy approached his mother telling her of that day's discussion. He asked her if she could explain the meaning of *integrity*. He knew the definition he explained, but wasn't really clear on what it meant.

The boy's mom suggested the boy visit his grandfather's store and ask grandpa for an interpretation. After all, she said, grandpa is in business, he'd surely be able to provide a good example of what integrity meant.

The next day the boy did as his mom suggested. Once the boy explained to his grandfather what he wanted to know, the grandfather said, "Suppose a nice lady comes into my store and buys an item that costs exactly $20 with tax. The lady hands me a twenty dollar bill and is walking out of the store. As I am putting the twenty in the cash drawer, I notice that in fact the lady has given me two twenty dollar bills. They were so new, they stuck together. This is where integrity comes in: Should I tell my partner?"

Webster's definition of integrity is "firm adherence to a code of especially moral or artistic values." Integrity is the way you were raised, the beliefs you hold sacred. I knew a man who worked in the warehouse of a large nationwide retailer. Among his duties was to unload truckloads of merchandise to be sold in the store. Occasionally, he explained, a bill of lading showed twelve of an item in a crate. However, after opening and counting the items inside he found thirteen or fourteen instead of the twelve shown on the bill. To his way of thinking, the extra items belonged to no one, so he would take the one or two extra items for his own use. I called it stealing. He disagreed. He called it extras, free. This man didn't think he was stealing. What do you think?

In a sales presentation, if you lie about a product or service, is it okay to do so because you're in sales? I know people who would not become a salesperson because it is their belief that to be a salesperson they would have to lie to people. I don't believe lying is a required function of a salesperson. Unfortunately, however, many salespeople believe it is, and worst, many prospects believe all salespeople lie. Of course, this becomes yet another obstacle a salesperson must overcome on the way to a sale.

The correct image in selling is both internal and external: how you see yourself, and how others see you. We have all heard the saying, "You only have one chance to make a first impression." The image you present is the first impression and is why correct image (CI) is first in the formula for success. Before you can effectively use planned positive action (PPA), the customer's mind must be open and receptive to the presentation to follow.

Remember, one cannot act in conflict with one's own self-image. If you believe you can succeed, you will. If you focus on the goal of success and believe you will reach that goal, you are in fact programming your personal computer to achieve the goal. Your brain is a goal-striving mechanism very much like a heat-seeking missile. If you lock in your goal, your brain will see to it that you get there. Your self-image will cause you to act like the sort of person you think you are and not allow you to act differently. Change your self-image, portray the correct image, and you'll change your life.

3

Visualize the Sale

Speaking of locking on to a goal. A by-product of Maxwell Maltz's study of the brain and its ability to lock in to a goal like a heat seeking missile is a technique widely used in sports clinics. The technique is called *visualization*. Visualization is taking advantage of the goal-striving characteristic of the brain coupled with the fact that your brain cannot differentiate between a real and an imagined experience.

Have you ever watched a hypnotist at work? After hypnotizing a subject, the hypnotist can suggest to the subject that the room is becoming colder and colder. The room is now below the freezing point. Because the subject is in a trance and under the influence of the hypnotist, the subject begins to shiver. Goose bumps begin to form on the subject's arms and body. This happens while it is actually 70 degrees in the room.

The reason this happens is because the subject's brain believes the programming it is receiving, that it is cold, and sends the normal signal to the extremities to shiver and develop goose bumps. The brain cannot differentiate what is real and what is suggested to be real.

This makes a good stage act, but because this fact exists about the brain, we can put it to good use. We can fool our brain into believing things that better serve our purpose. We can visualize a presentation over and over again, resulting in the prospect's saying yes and buying. Mental practice. Because it cannot differentiate practice from actual selling appointments, the brain causes us to be more confident in our ability to make a sale, resulting in a positive self-image. Resulting in more sales.

In his research, Maxwell Maltz concluded that because of the power of the personal computers housed in our brains and the programming we feed them, we cannot act in conflict with our self-image. This means that if you truly believe that you cannot do something, you can't. Your brain will see to it. If you constantly program your thinking to believe you cannot achieve a certain goal, your personal computer (brain) will receive your orders (programming) and carry out your wish. It is very much like a self-fulfilling prophecy. When you were in school, you or someone you knew said you were or he or she was not good at math. So you or they weren't. You will never be good at math unless you change the program to say, "I am good at math; I can do this." Your words or thoughts are programming input to your internal computer. Put in positive thoughts, and positive results are the output.

You can cause your brain to believe something good or something bad. Sometimes our brain is programmed externally. Someone else causes our brain to believe something good or something not so good. The following examples come from my experiences.

My son Jason has attention deficit disorder (ADD). As with most children with this disorder, school work, especially work that required lots of attention to detail, was difficult for Jason. In the fourth and fifth grades, Jason was doing miserably in math. After reading *Psycho-Cybernetics*, my wife, Debbie, and I began programming Jason's thinking about his ability to conquer math. As Jason struggled with math problems at the kitchen table at night, often throwing his hands up in disgust saying he couldn't do it, we would tell him he could. We told Jason that unlike for some children, math was something he could easily do. We told him that he had special skills that made learning math easy for him.

The change didn't happen overnight. However, over the years to follow, Jason conquered math. Today Jason is in college studying engineering. His easiest subject is math. Amazing, isn't it?

I seldom play golf anymore, but I still enjoy the times when I do. After studying self-image psychology, I reflected on the times I played and was at a water hazard on a golf course. Before this hole I played several holes that didn't have water on them, hitting the golf ball at least one hundred and fifty yards off the tee. Then I found myself at a water hazard. The farther edge was only seventy five yards away. I reached down into my golf bag in search of the oldest ball to tee up. I though to myself, I don't want to lose a brand new ball in the water, so I'll use an old one instead. Did I say "I'll use" or did I say "I'll lose" an old ball? It didn't matter which word I used, the meaning's the same.

As soon as I teed up that old ball, I mentally told my personal computer I planned to hit the ball into the water in front of me. The computer said okay, if that's what you want! When I swung the golf club, the computer commanded all the muscles and joints involved in the swing to hit the ball in a manner that would cause the ball to land in the water. My thoughts (input) produced a self-fulfilling prophecy (output), the ball in the water.

If I were a downhill ski racer, what do you think would happen if just before I started my run, I said to myself, "Gosh this is steep. I'm afraid I'll fall?" The chance of my falling would increase greatly. I'm not saying that we shouldn't recognize the difficulty of a particular situation. If, however, we focus on the potential for failure instead of the goal of success, the chances of failure increase.

I attribute a great deal of the success I've enjoyed in life to the programming my mother instilled in me. For as long as I can remember, my mother told me I could achieve anything I set my mind to. I'm sure my mother hadn't read books on psychology; however, she truly believed in the power of the mind. She felt this way in spite of the fact that she was a single mother rearing four children alone on the sweatshop wages she earned working in a dress factory in New York City. Because my mother believed so strongly in me, I believed in me. There was nothing I felt I could not do. My destiny was in my hands—under my control. I have a positive self-image, and have always viewed myself as having the ability to achieve any goal I set for myself.

Had I been programmed throughout my life as one who was doomed to fail—doomed to fail for economic, cultural, or racial reasons—my self-image might have been different. I may have developed a negative self-image. I say *may* have, instead of *would* have, because ultimately it is up to me to accept the negative programming. History has proved this point. People have succeeded in spite of constant negative programming aimed at them by their parents, peers, and society in general. In spite of it all, they rose above attempts to hold them down, and they achieved success. Even if you have been the victim of negative programming, it is never too late to reverse your self-image and begin to program yourself to achieve. You have a choice.

Correct Image + Planned Positive Action = Success On Purpose

4

Understand the Prospect's Objections and Concerns

As I travel the country conducting sales training seminars, I ask my sales trainees the following questions: "Why won't the prospect buy on the first visit?" and "What emotions, fears, apprehensions, and objections cause the prospect to delay a purchase?"

The following are the most common answers I hear:

1. The prospect wants to shop around.
2. Cost is more than expected.
3. The prospect wants to think about it.
4. The prospect does not trust the salesperson.
5. The prospect doesn't perceive a need.
6. The prospect is afraid to make a bad decision.

These emotions, fears, and objections are a wall between the salesperson and the prospect. Before we can expect the prospect to buy, we must climb over or knock down the wall that separates us.

EFFECTIVE SELLING SKILLS: OVERCOMING THE BUYER'S WALL OF RESISTANCE

Since childhood we have been programmed to resist a salesperson. That programming started immediately after the first phone call we answered when a telemarketer made what we thought to be an incredible offer, such as a free trip to Hawaii, a free television, or a free video cassette recorder. Our parents taught us that nothing is for nothing! Their parents taught them the same thing. Beware the sales pitch! Salespeople try to separate you from your money! In many instances our parents and their parents were right.

Most people go through life harboring a basic distrust of salespeople. As salespeople we have to recognize and understand this basic truth. We have to learn to deal with these emotions. We can't simply ignore them. We have to learn to work with them.

Although people distrust salespeople, they want to be sold. That is an axiom. They appreciate the talents of a professional salesperson. They dislike a bumbling salesperson. People are afraid to make decisions because they are afraid to be wrong. No one looks forward to making a bad decision and running the risk of ridicule. Unless people know a great deal about a subject, the indecisiveness is often due to fear—the fear of making a mistake in life.

Recognizing that prospects' decisions to buy are affected by the psychological programming they have received since they were children, we must develop methods systematically to eliminate those fears. The decision to buy must become either automatic or at least easier to make. Let's analyze each objection so we can understand how to handle them.

We're going to shop around.

All too often your prospect does not know how much your product should cost. Not long ago, a national survey was conducted to determine the general public's awareness of alarm systems. The results of the survey revealed that less than 5 percent of the people contacted knew the name of one alarm company. When given the name of one of the largest and oldest alarm companies, less than 8 percent knew in which business the company was engaged. The average consumer knows little about alarm systems.

In my years in the alarm business, I have met prospects who before my presentation perceived the value of an alarm system to be $5,000. In the same neighborhood I met people with a similar socioeconomic background and education who perceived the value of an alarm system to be $300. The plain fact is that most prospects do not have a clue about a fair price. Is it any wonder their first reaction is to want to shop around? Of course not. Does that mean we can't close that sale now? No, it doesn't. We can close the sale immediately, and I'll show you how.

When shopping around, from how many companies should a prospect obtain estimates? If you were to conduct a worldwide survey, you'd find the winning answer to be three. Why three? Who made that rule? Even the U.S. government uses that rule. Three would make sense if three represented a good sampling of a given market, but three appears to be the rule when there are twelve companies who provide the product or service or when there are two hundred.

I didn't expect it to cost that much.
Another company is willing to sell a similar
product for less.

I'm not surprised a prospect doesn't know how much my product costs. Perceived or known value varies according to how much or how little the prospect has been exposed to the product. I am not at all surprised by their feeling they could find a similar product for less money. There will always be products similar to the one you are selling that can be purchased for less money. It is the salesperson's job to build perceived value in the product he or she sells.

When a prospect believes your product is too expensive, it is usually because you didn't do a good enough job building value by selling features and benefits or because the prospect started with a low perceived value of your product. Earlier I wrote that I have met prospects whose perceived value of an alarm system was $5,000 before I started my presentation. Because my average system sale is less than $3,000 and as long as I don't make a fool of myself and destroy the demonstration, price or objection to the price is not a problem with this prospect. However, if a prospect's perceived value is $300 at the beginning of the presentation, and my average sale is just under $3,000, I have a lot of value building to do.

One of the steps to successful selling is to build perceived value. If when you're finished presenting your product, the prospect's perceived value has grown to an amount equal to or greater than the price of your product, your chances of making the sale today improve. If on the other hand, when you complete your presentation the prospect's perceived value is lower than the price you quoted, your chances of selling today diminish. You may have a price problem or objection at the end of the presentation. Does that make sense?

Of course one presupposes that you know your product backward and forward and that you know your competitors' products as well. One also presupposes that you have been trained or have sat down with pen in hand and listed all the features and benefits of your product over competitors' products and have practiced your presentation.

Do you believe your product is worth the price you are asking for it? If you don't, find out why it is worth more, or sell something else.

We never make snap decisions.
We always take time to think things over.

For many salespeople, this is the toughest objection to overcome. In my sales classes, when I hear the think it over objection, I can't help but tell the following story.

> One day a couple, Jim and Mary, went to a family reunion barbeque at a family member's home. As was the custom, each couple would prepare part of the meal. This time Mary's job was to prepare the ham. Mary had a reputation for fixing delicious hams. Mary was in the kitchen when Jim walked in. Jim noticed that Mary chopped off one end of the ham, turned it around, and chopped off the other end. Jim asked, "Why did you do that? Is it because the meat is sweeter in the center? Or is it because the meat is fattier on the ends?" Mary thought about the question for a moment and said, "Well, I don't know exactly. My mother always cut the ends off and I guess that's why I do. However, I'm sure," she said, "it's for a good reason."
>
> After Mary put the ham in the oven, she walked into the living room where her mother was sitting and asked, "Why do we cut the ends off the ham?" Everyone was now looking at Mary's mother. After some thought she said, "You know, I don't know! I think it's because grandma always did and I learned to cook from her." The mystery was getting deeper. Jim, Mary, Mary's mother, and several of the relatives who had heard Mary ask the question walked into the yard in search of Grandma. The whole entourage found Grandma sitting on a lawn chair in the yard. Mary's mother explained that Jim had asked Mary, and Mary had asked her, and, "Now we need to ask you. Why did you cut both ends off the ham before you cooked it?" Grandma looked at everyone as if they were nuts and said, "Because I only had a pan this big, the whole ham wouldn't fit."

I know it's a long story to make a point, but it makes the point as well as anything I've heard. Sometimes people say they want to think it over and don't know why. Some people always sleep on decisions and haven't a clue why they do it. But if they asked mom and dad, grandma and grandpa, they'd probably find it's because of a lifelong habit. People generally don't trust their own ability to make good decisions. Deferring a decision is safe.

Everyone knows someone who was roped into a bad deal. We have all received phone calls offering unbelievable deals. Our parents told us to beware! Don't believe salespeople! Their job is to separate you from your money! So we have been conditioned, (programmed). It's the salesperson's job to build trust and belief. If prospects trust you and believe you, they will buy from you.

Another reason a prospect says, "We're going to think about it" is to hide the real objection (a smoke screen). Many prospects don't like to tell you they think your price is too high. They would rather not say they have a problem with you, your company, or your product. It is much easier to say, "We're going to think it over." However, after you leave, Mr. Prospect says to Mrs. Prospect, "Do you believe the price we're expected to pay? Is the salesperson nuts or just think we're nuts?"

Do you think this customer will call back? I don't think so. If you have ever heard the saying "buyers are liars," this is why it is so. Buyers may lie to you when they think the truth would be more painful for you or them.

For example, suppose a couple, after ten years of living in one home, is considering redecorating. The husband believes that decorating would cost four to five thousand dollars, and his wife believes it will cost six to ten thousand dollars. This happens, doesn't it? A situation in which the prospects have different buying levels? Sure it does.

As it turns out, the wife happens to know someone who knows someone who knows an interior decorator who is very good. The wife arranges to have the decorator come to the home to meet with the couple to discuss the project.

After interviewing the couple and walking through their home drawing rough sketches, the decorator leaves to research the project. The decorator explains that an appointment will be made to discuss the findings. Let's further suppose that the decorator returns and makes the presentation. As the husband and wife listen and look over the drawings and samples the decorator put together, they are both impressed. Now comes the moment of truth. The decorator informs the couple that the decorating plan just presented can be completed for only $23,650. If you were the prospect, what would you say?

If you were blown away by the price, you probably would tell the decorator a lie. You'd probably say you want to sleep on it; talk it over; think about it. Anything but the truth.

The truth is painful. To tell the truth, you would either have to admit you couldn't afford to spend that much or say you didn't think the job was worth that much. It is much easier to say you want to think it over. If the salesperson believes you really want to think it over and leaves, chances are slim he or she will ever make the sale. If, however, the salesperson pursues the reason for thinking it over, attempting to uncover the reason for the delay, you just might tell the truth: it costs too much; it's more than you wanted to spend; it's more than you can afford. With those facts, it is possible for the decorator to modify the plan.

How much time do you assume the prospect wants to think it over? When I ask this question in my sales clinics, the answer usually is a couple of days or more. Try this thought on for size. The next time your prospects say they want to think it over, don't assume they mean days. Assume they mean minutes. Make up a reason to go to your car and say the following:

"I can understand your need to think and talk it over. My spouse and I often do the same. I have to get something from my car, so while I'm doing that, it will be a perfect opportunity for the two of you to talk this over. I'll be back in a few minutes." Get up and head for the door. If they don't stop you, they only need minutes, not days, to talk it over. Have the guts to try this and you will be pleasantly surprised by the results.

Trust is a psychological motivator to buy or not to buy.

In the previous paragraph, I wrote that your customer must trust you and believe you in order to buy from you. Although this may not be true 100 percent of the time, it is true most of the time. In fact, I believe that after need is established, that is, the customer is sure that he or she needs and wants your product or service, trust becomes the most important obstacle.

Let's evaluate the impact of trust. Would you agree, if a prospect needed and wanted a product or service, and if a relative whom they liked and respected could provide the product or service, the prospect would most likely buy from the relative without even calling anyone else? I believe, more often than not, the relative would get the business. Why? The answer is simple . . . trust. If I trust you, I believe you. If I believe you and trust you, then I believe you when you say that your product is the best for me. If I trust and believe you, then I believe you when you say that the price you are charging me is a fair and equitable investment. On the other hand, if I don't trust you or you haven't earned my trust yet, I'm not sure I believe you when you say your product and price are the best. I may want to check with other companies to compare. In other words, compare so I can check your honesty.

Salespeople must do all they can do to earn prospects' trust. A salesperson can earn and develop a prospect's trust with consistent use of the sales steps explained later in this book.

I don't think I need your product or service.

Unless it's a steal, why buy something you don't need? Another requirement of a presentation is to create need. Your prospects may not know enough to know they have a problem. In the security business, it is important to be sure that the prospect needs security for the right reasons. For example, it is not unusual for alarm system prospects to purchase a security system to keep burglars from stealing their possessions, such as a VCR, stereo, television, and jewelry. However, from a sales standpoint, it is better if the prospect's primary need is life safety. With full-replacement insurance policies, the prospect can rationalize that an inexpensive alarm system is good enough. Should the prospect suffer a loss, insurance would fully replace the stolen goods. Although this is true, the trauma of a burglary is far worse then the loss. I've interviewed burglary victims who have told me that the burglary so affected them that they threw away undergarments after the burglary because they felt the burglar's hands when they wore them.

I've been told about fourteen-year-old boys and girls who felt so insecure after a burglary that for the first time in many years, they were afraid to sleep in their own rooms. They wanted to climb in bed with their parents. Insurance does not replace peace of mind. Both burglaries occurred when no one was home. The problem is far worse when someone is at home during a burglary.

It is the salesperson's job to teach the prospect about the true problem, emphasizing life safety and peace of mind. If the presentation does not properly address these issues, the salesperson is taking the risk that the prospect is not fully aware of the problems or of the need for a solution.

When I was a salesman for NCR, the primary product I sold was NCR's line of cash registers. That was many years ago, but even then, most retail stores owned some type of cash register, and more often then not, it was an NCR. However, as technology advanced, driven by customer need, older registers were becoming or were past being obsolete. Many of the retail merchants who were proud owners of the older technology did not always perceive the need to discard the old register in favor of a new one. It was my job as a salesman to find prospects with older technology and persuade them to upgrade to the new technology.

The important change in NCR's "new" technology in my day was to departmentalize sales and track sales by employees. The reason was twofold. First, by departmentalizing sales, it was easier to determine profit by merchandize type. Second, and more important, the new register helped control employee theft. We all have seen reports on shoplifting and the eventual cost to the consumer because of this problem. However, shoplifting pales in comparison to inside employee theft. The same was true in the 1960s, when I worked for NCR.

My problem then was that retail merchants did not always perceive a need to control employee theft. They were convinced their employees were honest and would never steal from them. Of course, some employees were stealing; that was documented. However, it was never the employees of the merchant I was calling on. This is a classic case of the psychological law of self-exception: "It won't happen to me." Thus it was my job to open the prospect's eyes to the possibility of a problem before the need arose and by opening eyes to make a sale.

Here is one of the ways I reached my goal. When speaking with the prospect, I would pose the following hypothetical situation.

> Suppose a young man, approximately nineteen years of age, good looking, and clean cut, came into your store. Suppose you were busy servicing another customer when the young man said to you, "Mister, I can see you're busy, and I want to purchase this merchandise which costs five dollars with tax. I have a ten dollar bill." He shows you the bill. "Because you're busy," the young man says, "I'll just put this ten in your register and take a five as my change, okay?" My question to you, Mr. Prospect, is would you allow him to open your cash register and take his own change?

The merchants always answered, "absolutely not" and "no way!" I would ask "why not?" The merchants would say, "because the kid could take more than he should, he might steal from me."

I'd continue. "Mr. Prospect, let's push that hypothetical situation a bit further."

> You place an ad in the newspaper and a sign on your store window. A young man answers the ad who looks just like the one in the first scenario. After interviewing

him and giving him an addition test and whatever other test you might have him take, you decide to hire him. Will you let him open your cash register now?

My job was to cause the prospect to question his judgment, to climb out of his paradigm and look at reality. Anyone can be a thief, even people we like and trust. People are only as honest as the system in which they live and work allows them to be. If enough temptation is dangled, borderline dishonest people will grab the bait.

If I was successful, the prospect now perceived a need for a solution to the potential problem of inside theft. Of course, I sold a product that solved the problem.

There is a lesson to be learned here. Prospects do not always perceive a need for your product. That does not mean they do not need your product. They don't know they have a problem. Don't cave in and quit when you hear, "I don't need it." You're not doing yourself or the prospect any favors when you quit.

The fear of making a bad decision is another "sale stopper." No one looks forward to the ridicule and embarrassment that could follow the decision to purchase a product that to everyone else appears stupid.

Just think of how the people who bought an Edsel automobile felt a couple of years later. How about the people who bought a product or service the day before the big expose on television.

It's that fear, the fear of being considered foolish; or having thrown away money on a worthless or overrated product that worries people. The easy decision is to say NO.

Now that we have identified some of the objections, Chapter 5 discusses how to structure a presentation to overcome them.

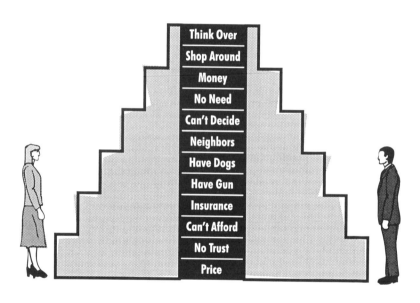

5

The Six-Step Selling Plan

The first obstacle to overcome is the lack of trust. If customers don't trust me, they won't believe me when I try to persuade them they need my services. When I was selling security, too many prospects just did not believe that anyone would ever try to burglarize their home. They felt this way even though houses like theirs, in the same neighborhood, owned by people like them were burglarized.

I was told by one of the greatest sales trainers I have met, Mitch Resnick, that most people suffer from a condition called the *psychological law of self exception*. Adherents to this law state, "I won't have a problem, someone else will or could, but not me." This is an absolute law that works in a number of arenas.

For example, a smoker continues to smoke despite all warnings from the medical community. If smokers knew for sure that if they were to smoke after today they would contract cancer, they would quit today. Most people believe smoking does increase the risk of contracting cancer. However, smokers under the influence of the psychological law of self exception believe it won't happen to them. For this same reason some of my prospects believed they would not have a burglary or fire problem. I knew better.

During my alarm sales career, a high percentage of customers to whom I sold alarm systems bought only after they were burglarized. It was like closing the barn door after the horse was out. I saw first hand the emotions they experienced—emotions that ranged from total fear to rage. I've known people who have moved from a house they loved because they were burglarized and no longer felt safe there. They couldn't sleep. They became ill. These emotional experiences had little to do with stolen possessions. The emotional pain was caused by loss of peace of mind. They no longer felt safe in that house. I've had burglary victims tell me they felt personally violated, as if they had been raped.

When prospects tell me they don't need a security alarm system, I know better and believe it is my job to persuade them they do. I'm willing to bet that every burglary victim would like to roll the clock back in time and have someone like me talk them into an alarm system rather than go through the emotional experience of a burglary.

An interesting example of need was demonstrated to me when I sold for National Cash Register (NCR). In early 1970 I was selected by NCR to sell a revolutionary new product called the Electra Bar. The Electra Bar was the first of its kind automatic liquor dispensing and register system. When the server depressed the appropriate key on the cash register, the exact amount of liquor required was dispensed into a glass, the liquor was subtracted from inventory, and the predetermined sales price for the drink was added to the patron's bill. The advantage of the system included strict inventory control and control against employee theft.

Persuading bar owners that they needed this product was the challenge. I would demonstrate that if ten quarts of liquor were poured each day and the bartender only overpoured by the thickness of the line on a shot glass, at the retail price of $1.50 per drink, the merchant would lose $10,000 per year in retail value. Of course, reality was that servers overpoured much more than the thickness of the line, not to mention the drinks they gave away to induce a tip and the money they simply stole.

As Earl Nightingale once said, "Sometimes you have to get prospects to smell the flowers before they will believe they will die." To sell a system that would control loss, I had to get the prospect to believe me, to believe they had a problem that needed solving.

However, to get prospects to believe me, I had to start working on getting them to trust me. I had got to get them to like me a little more.

What I have done so far is explain the wall we often encounter. That is, the emotional wall the prospects erect between themselves and the salesperson. It is the salesperson's job to find a way to overcome or climb that wall. I call the wall *the buyer's wall of resistance*. To climb that wall, we start with step one.

STEP ONE: SELL WARM-UP

Over the past years, I have accompanied hundreds of salespeople on sales presentations. On all too many of these calls I have witnessed the salesperson skip the warm-up altogether and get right to business. After the presentation, when I asked them why they skipped this step, their answer was usually something like this: "I don't feel comfortable doing a warm-up." "It's just not me." I can understand that feeling. This step comes easier to some than to others. However, I'm convinced that everyone can be taught to conduct a sincere warm-up.

What Is a Warm-up? How Is It Done?

Everyone has something they are proud of or something they like to talk about. They usually display what they like to talk about in a prominent place so visitors can and will see it. For example, my wife Debbie and I love to sail and race sailboats. If you are a

1. Sell Warm-Up

Think Over
Shop Around
Money
No Need
Can't Decide
Neighbors
Have Dogs
Have Gun
Insurance
Can't Afford
No Trust
Price

Figure 5-1 The Buyer's Wall of Resistance

salesperson and you are in my home more than three minutes and haven't figured that out, you just haven't been looking. We have sailing trophies, pictures of sailboats, and various sailing magazines. An observant salesperson would pick up on that and in the warm-up step say, "Do you folks like to sail?" Whereupon we would respond. Then the salesperson would ask, "Why did you select that particular type of boat?" And we would begin telling him our sailing life story.

All it takes to warm people are a few probing questions about a subject they like to talk about. When they start telling you about what they enjoy, they begin to relax and you begin to become a friend. When they like you, they want to trust you.

As a salesperson, it is important that you learn to become more observant. If there are pictures of family members on the wall, they were put there to be noticed. Go up to them and look at them. What are they telling you? Are different people featured in the pictures, or do you notice the same person over and over again, such as a child with a baseball bat in one and a picture of the child at third base in another. You can believe that someone is proud of their Little League baseball player. You should ask, "Is this a picture of one of your children?" "Really!" "Is he still playing?" "With whom?" "What position does he play?" "Has he won any awards?" "Really!" "Do you have the trophies here?"

If you show genuine interest the prospects will begin to open up. Take the time to do this. Your investment in time will be returned many times over in commission checks.

STEP TWO: SELL YOURSELF

When you have developed a bit of rapport with your prospects, they are more conditioned to listen to you. If you have a background in your field of sales and if your expertise has anything to do with the satisfaction level of your prospects (and in most cases it does), then it is in your best interest to tell prospects why they should want to do business with you as an individual. Believe it or not, most prospects don't consider the salesperson an important ingredient in the overall product or service they purchase. We know better. In the security business, for example, the difference between a system that works well and one that becomes a nuisance to the customer and, possibly worse, a false-alarm monster can be the expertise level of the salesperson.

Salespeople in the security alarm business are called *security consultants*. The consultant's expertise as a system designer is key to customer satisfaction. The consultant's sales ability to persuade prospects to buy quality security with the right amount and type of security devices has everything to do with customers' future satisfaction with their alarm system. Because a security system can be a life-saving system, customers' lives can ride on the design and on the sales ability of the security consultant. In this light, it easily can be seen how the sales consultant's expertise is important. Therefore, the consultant needs to establish his or her credibility early in the presentation.

Every field of sales is similar in some ways. It is the salesperson's job to persuade the prospect to buy the right product and to pay the right price. When customers buy junk, they blame the company and the salesperson. When they buy good quality, customers take the credit for being an astute buyer.

The First Impression

You have only one chance to make a first impression. From the moment you arrive at the appointment you must begin to score positive points rather than negative points. Your first opportunity to gain or lose is based on how prompt you are. If you are late for an appointment you have begun with negative points that you may not be able to overcome. Just think as if you're the one who is waiting for a salesperson to arrive. Perhaps you made this appointment at the specific time you did because you had other plans afterward. When the salesperson is late you begin a slow burn. You become aware of the time lost and become irritated and on edge. When the salesperson finally does arrive you already don't like him or her. You don't notice any of the other things the salesperson is doing that are designed to score points in his or her favor. The salesperson not only fails to gain points because the prospect is preoccupied by anger but also loses valuable points for being late.

Be on time or a little early. Vince Lombardi, the late coach of the Green Bay Packers football team, in the film *Second Effort* spoke about this subject and coined a phrase, "Lombardi time." Lombardi time is fifteen minutes ahead. The coach recommended that salespeople set their watches fifteen minutes fast and leave them that way. I have kept my watch fifteen minutes fast since then. The point is that it is better and easier to apologize for being early than for being late. When you are early, prospects often say, "My, you're prompt" and you have scored points —Lombardi sales points. Remember, they add up to Lombardi sales touchdowns.

If you want to be professional, you must dress like a professional. It is easier to apologize for being overdressed than to suffer the point loss of being underdressed. People naturally respect a man or a woman dressed in a business suit. He or she looks more important. Have you ever seen an executive in causal

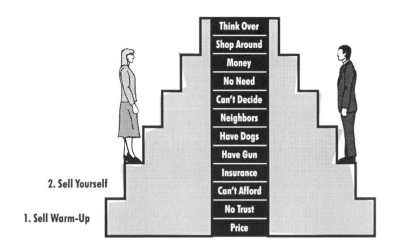

Figure 5-2   The Buyer's Wall of Resistance

clothes when you were accustomed to seeing him or her in a suit? That person looks different—not as important or as impressive as he or she did in a suit. You want prospects to look upon you as a professional, like their doctor, lawyer, or accountant. They usually respect their doctor's opinion about their health and you want them to respect your opinion about their needs.

I can't count how many times I've had a salesperson tell me that in Anytown, people don't want the salesperson to dress in a suit and tie. I've even had some try to persuade me that they would lose sales if they wore a suit. That's pure bunk! I have never lost a sale because I looked professional. It is far easier to become relaxed looking if the prospect insists than it is to dress up if you are dressed casually. The fact is many salespeople would rather not dress in a suit. They prefer the casual feel. But remember, when you are on sales calls you are at work. The uniform for work in the sales field is a well-tailored business suit.

Take control of the appointment. Although you are in a prospect's home, it is your show. That's the professional way. Taking initial control is as easy as selecting the place where you want this meeting to take place. I prefer the kitchen table. The kitchen table is where people sit with friends. The formal living room is where they bring strangers. I want them to consider me their friend, so I suggest the kitchen table as the area to show my products.

Another reason to choose the kitchen table over the dining room table is the value of the table itself. The last thing I want to do is set a demonstration kit, brief case, or anything else down on a beautiful dining room table. If I did, the prospect could be worried about potential scratches and not pay attention to what I'm saying. I need their undivided attention. I don't need distractions. Even when you sit at the kitchen table, I recommend you carry a soft placemat to place under your demonstration case before setting it on the table. Even if it's an old table, prospect's appreciate your concern for their property. I was once told by an architect when walking through a historic building surveying for a security system, "Old cracks are historic, new cracks are a disaster." The same applies to old tables. Old scratches hold memories, new scratches are a disaster and a sale killer.

STEP THREE: SELL YOUR COMPANY

A Ford is a Ford is a Ford. Or is it? If it is, why should I care where I buy it? Many customers do not instinctively know it is important from which company they buy, but of course it is important. On the other side of the fence, I have found that many salespeople representing a large, well-established, reputable company did not tell the prospect about the company. They assumed the prospects already knew all about the company and still worse that prospects would appreciate the benefits they would receive by buying from this great company.

I'm sure you have all seen the word *assume* broken down. Don't make an *ass* out of *u* and *me*. Tell prospects why they should want to buy the product from you and what the benefit will be to them. It is important to accomplish this step without knocking your competition. When you point your finger at someone or something else, you have four fingers pointing back at you.

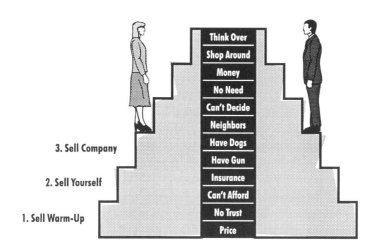

Figure 5-3   The Buyer's Wall of Resistance

I can only make three fingers point back at me, but the point is made. People don't like to hear you bum rap your competition. You have heard the expression from *Hamlet* that one "doth protest too much, methinks." When you knock your competitor, prospects begin to wonder why you are so worried about that particular competitor. They begin to wonder if you're not three to four times worse than the competitor you knock. Four fingers point back. Methinks thou protest too much! So don't do it.

How many years has your company been in business? If your company is relatively new, how many years have you been in the industry? How long have other members of your firm been in business? Add them together. The total is your years in business. For example, suppose you have been in the industry for three years, your top employee for three years, your partner for three years, and another staff member for two years. The total experience is eleven years. Therefore, you can say your organization has more than ten years of experience.

Your job as salesperson is to separate yourself and your company from the competition to make your company special in your prospect's eyes. The best way to do that is to sell yourself and your company's features, advantages, and benefits. When you do this in a highly professional manner, you simply elevate yourself. It is up to your competitors to come up to your level, if they can.

To prepare for your next presentation, sit down, take out a piece of paper, and list all the reasons a prospect would benefit by buying from your company. List the features about your company that should impress your prospect. Practice this portion of your presentation over and over until the words come smoothly and easily.

Go through what you have written and look for *spears*. Spears are words or statements you make that sound good to you but can hurt you if the customer takes them the wrong way. For example, I worked with a salesperson in the alarm business who, when telling the customer about his background, said the following:

> My career in the alarm business started 10 years ago when I was hired by a company called ABC. I worked for them for several years, advancing to commercial alarm specialist. I then moved to a company called DEF. After two years with them I made a career change and went to work for GHI Company and now work for JKL Company.

The salesperson was attempting to show the prospect that he was not a rookie, that he had several years of alarm consulting experience. However, there were two important spear groups in his presentation. First, the prospect might feel that the salesperson moves around too much and wonder where that salesperson is going to be if and when the buyer has a problem in the future. Second, the prospect may not have heard of ABC Company or any of the other companies. Thanks to the salesperson, the prospect now has the name of several other companies to call to get system prices. It is possible that the customer hadn't even considered shopping around. However, she now thinks she should at the very least get a price from each of the companies the sales-

Figure 5-4   Don't Get Stuck with Any Spear Points!

person was so kind to mention. Get the point? Be careful not to get stuck with any spear points.

Look for spears in your presentation. Ask yourself if what you say can hurt you. If it can, you're throwing spears. Some salespeople throw a spear and then run out and try to catch it. Sometimes they catch it and all is okay. Sometimes they catch it in the heart. Make sure that what you are saying isn't a spear throw. Spear catching can be and often is fatal to your sales health.

STEP FOUR: DETERMINE THE NEED

Now that you have made them like you, have sold them on your value to them, and have sold them on the benefits that will accrue to them by doing business with your company, it is time to give the prospects a chance to speak. Everything you have done thus far has been to set their minds at ease, to relax them, and to increase their confidence in you. At this point, they should be more willing to level with you regarding their needs and desires. With the help of written, planned questions you can most assuredly determine their dominant buying motive (DBM).

I prefer using a written, survey-type questionnaire. The questions I ask serve two purposes: first to uncover the dominant buying motive and second to plant a seed. As human beings, we often hide our fear and insecurities in our subconscious. It is my job as a sales consultant to bring that fear to the conscious mind. The problem doesn't go away; it simply is stored in a place where the prospect doesn't have to face it everyday. However, it's still there.

Develop questions that attack the root of the problem your product is designed to solve. If you sell computers, ask questions about the current system and the problems the prospects have with it. Find out what the system does not do. Find the weakness and emphasize it. Have the courage to ask the questions you put on your list. Don't answer them for the prospect.

Questions asked should be designed to awaken prospects' subconscious about a problem that has not gone away but only been repressed. The prospects have stopped thinking about the problems and over a period of time have buried it in their subconscious minds.

It has been said by Maxwell Maltz that, "When logic comes in conflict with emotions, emotions will always win." We buy with our emotions and then justify our purchases with logic. Logic tells us we should do lots of things we don't do. When our emotions say yes, however, we say yes. Our lives are full of examples of this truth. Have you ever purchased a new car even though you already had a car that worked? You justified your decision by saying to yourself that the car is getting older and will certainly begin giving you trouble soon. (Twenty-five thousand dollars worth of trouble? I don't think so.) Therefore you have to buy the new car. Clothes, jewelry, houses, boats, and recreational equipment are purchased with emotions rather than logic.

If we know that people react emotionally not logically, it follows that we should sell to their emotional side. Sell to their

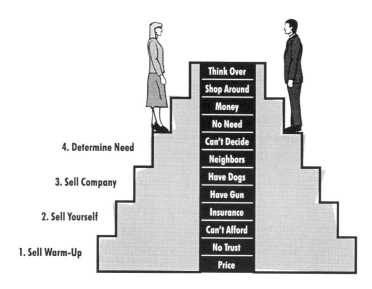

Figure 5-5   The Buyer's Wall of Resistance

emotions and prospects will justify their decision with logic. Demonstrate how the quality of prospects' lives will improve. The heavy burden they have been carrying in their subconscious will disappear and they will feel noticeably better.

Several years ago, a company I worked for rented a booth at the local home and garden show, which was held in a convention hall. The show was an annual event that was well attended and therefore very successful to the exhibitors. After the show ended, I received a call from someone with whom I talked at the show. "Mr. Jones" made an appointment for me to come to his home a couple days later to talk to his wife and him about an alarm system. I arrived at the home at the time scheduled. Mr. Jones answered the door, and before he moved out of the way so I could get in, he said:

> Now listen to me carefully. I don't want an alarm system. I personally don't think I need one and it annoys me to no end to think of spending money for an alarm system.

However, my wife wants one. She's convinced she needs one, and I am going to buy one for her. Do you understand me?

I said, "Yes, sir," and he let me in.

Mrs. Jones was waiting for us in the family room. Although the start of the meeting was somewhat unusual, the rest of the presentation went well as usual. At the conclusion, Mr. Jones signed the order form for a system to be installed a couple weeks later.

About a week after the installation I returned to the home, as was my custom, to review the system and its operations with the customers. A week is a sufficient amount of time for a new client to use the system, develop questions, and be ready to learn more. The follow-up visit is also a great time to ask for additional leads. I arrived at the appointed time, and Mr. Jones met me at the door as he did on my first visit. This time he was much friendlier. He invited me to his family room and offered me a beer. Before Mrs. Jones entered the room, Mr. Jones said:

You know I didn't want this system. The only reason I bought it was to make my wife happy. However, I don't know why, but since this system has been installed I just feel better. I don't know why, but I just do. The alarm system has given me peace of mind. I just wanted you to know that.

That wasn't the first or the last time someone has said the alarm system I sold them gave them peace of mind. It was an important happening for me. Here was a macho-type man who didn't want a system and within a week felt better because of the system. Peace of mind is an emotional, almost undefinable feeling. This man was afraid, as we all are. However, over the years he had hidden the fear in his subconscious. It was only after he was protected and the fear went away that he noticed the difference in the way he felt. What Mr. Jones experienced can be compared with always having a minor toothache to which you've grown accustomed over a period of time and hardly notice.

However, if all of a sudden the pain goes away, you feel noticeably better. That's the way it was with Mr. Jones. The pain was the threat of someone sneaking into his home while he slept.

STEP FIVE: SELL THE PROBLEM

If a prospect calls for an estimate on your product, don't assume he's considering the purchase for the right reasons. In many cases, prospects are considering the purchase of a system to prevent the loss of possessions. They don't want their jewelry, tools, furs, or stereo equipment stolen. They want to protect themselves, but deep inside, they really don't believe anything will happen to them. This form of denial is known as the *psychological law of self exception*; that is, "It's not going to happen to me."

It's important that prospects consider an alarm system for the right reason—protection of life. Nothing in the home is more valuable than the owners' lives. The lives and well-being of the children are far and away the priority. Once prospects realize it is their family that the system must protect, nothing but the best is good enough. They won't settle for second best.

Be prepared to discuss the types of criminal from whom homeowners must be protected. I discuss the following types:

- The professional: a cat burglar, usually after big scores
- The vandal: destroys homes on a dare, out of hate, or for the thrill
- The sex offender: preys mostly on women and children
- The drug addict: average habit more than $300 every day

You must vividly depict each of these types in your presentation. Make these criminals come alive using word pictures. Don't assume prospects are aware about how these criminals work. Educate them.

Use the FBI *Uniform Crime Report* statistics to make a point. To obtain a copy of the *Uniform Crime Report*, write to: The U.S. Department of Justice, Federal Bureau of Investigation, and ask for a copy of the *1992 Uniform Crime Report*.

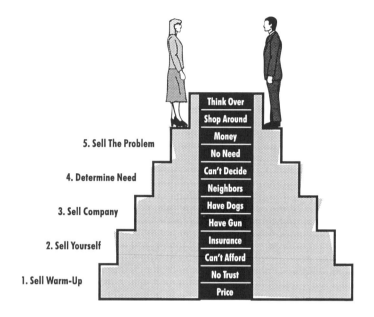

Figure 5-6   The Buyer's Wall of Resistance

The crime clock can be extremely effective. Don't be the wrong kind of nice person by being afraid to frighten prospects by telling about criminals. You are not making this stuff up. These type of criminals do exist. They are a real threat to your prospects and their well-being. You owe it to prospects to make them acutely aware of the presence and habits of criminals. You also present a more professional image when you educate customers. Their knowledge is not complete when it comes to the subject of crime, even if they have been a victim. It does not take long in the alarm business for you to become an authority. Share your knowledge with your prospects. You owe it to them and they will respect you for doing so.

STEP SIX: SELL THE SOLUTION

Once you have determined the prospects' needs and desires, you can aim your presentation at the problem they perceive they have. You can also focus on the problems that have surfaced from their subconsciousness. You should use word pictures in your presentation that confront the problems prospects have and then show them how your product solves or eliminates the problems. For example, to a prospect whose children come home at 3 P.M. and are home alone until approximately 5:30 P.M., I would say:

> Let's suppose it is 3 P.M. and your children have just arrived home from school. The children go into the house and lock the door. Let's further suppose that a burglar has chosen your home to burglarize. The burglar finds a concealed entry point, let's say the back door, which is in the den. He pries open the door using a crow bar that he inserts between the door and the door jamb. With the crow bar still in his hand, the burglar walks across the den in search of your valuables. At the same time, your son or daughter walks into the den and meets the burglar. What just happened is called an *accidental confrontation*. Nothing good comes from this type of chance meeting. That's what could happen without an XYZ Alarm System protecting your family.
>
> With our XYZ Alarm System at work, the following would happen. When the burglar applies pressure on the lock of the den door and the door swings open, the alarms sound immediately on the outside and the inside, scaring the intruder away. At the same time, a signal is transmitting to XYZ's 24-hour alarm-monitoring dispatch center, and the police are on their way. Let me ask you a question, Mrs. Prospect, "wouldn't you feel more comfortable with your children at home alone knowing that they are protected by XYZ's Latchkey Child Program? Of course you would."

Could what I just described happen? Can anyone tell me or the prospects that it won't happen? Of course it can happen and does. We don't know when tragedy will strike. All we can do is be prepared. Owning and properly using a quality alarm system can reduce this problem.

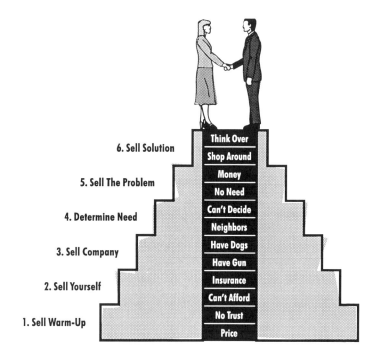

Figure 5-7   The Buyer's Wall of Resistance

When presenting your product—the solution—to the prospect, the golden rule to keep in mind is K.I.S.S. Keep it simple and smart. Keep it simple. Don't confuse prospects with the technical features of your product. Tell them what they want to know. Tell them what your product will do for them and how they will benefit.

REMEMBER K.I.S.S.

In 1969 I attended a seminar put on by Ira Hayes. Ira is a public speaker who spoke at seminars for NCR. Ira used an analogy on the K.I.S.S. formula that I've never forgotten. His analogy went this way:

When someone goes to a store to purchase a TV, do you think he wants to know what makes a T.V. work? I don't think so. As a matter of fact, to this day, I still don't completely understand how you can plug a TV in a normal wall electrical outlet, add some rabbit ears for an antenna, turn the knob to channel three, and see a beautiful color picture. Then, when you simply turn a dial, the TV displays another channel and you see a different picture. I don't understand how that happens. It's magic. However, do you want to know something? I really don't care. When I buy a television I don't want anyone to tell me how a picture gets there. Tell me about the quality of the picture; tell me about the remote control and how it will simplify my life; tell me that it is a color set, but don't tell me how it happens. All the explanation will do is confuse me. I might think I have to know all that in order to use the TV.

I heard what Ira was saying; however, I apparently didn't understand what he said. A year or so later, I learned the meaning of K.I.S.S. the hard way.

At the time I was a successful senior sales representative with NCR. I earned the coveted C.P.C. pin for the second straight year and was at the NCR convention. As was normally the case, the conventions served as the forum to introduce and release new and exciting products. This year was to be no exception. An NCR executive from headquarters addressed the attendees and announced the release of the first ever electronic calculator. He had one with him on stage. The calculator was about the size of a fax machine today. Besides having two memories, it added, subtracted, multiplied, and determined square root. To demonstrate, the executive held the calculator in one hand and with the other entered *12 × 12 =* . At the blink of an eye the answer *144* appeared on the screen. For those of you who weren't adults at the time, this may not seem spectacular. You have to realize that at the time, the only way to multiply with a calculating machine was to use a complicated formula of stepover multiplication on an adding machine or to use a Monroe Friden calculator, which we nicknamed "the chug-a-chug machine." The reason for the nickname was that if you multiplied twelve times twelve on the Monroe machine, the carriages on top would start moving in opposite directions toward each other making a *chug-a-chug-a-chug-a-chug* sound. After awhile, one could obtain the answer *144* by reading part of carriage A and part of carriage B. Reading an answer was like reading a slide rule. Calculation was also extremely slower than with an electronic machine. However, before this convention, electronic calculators did not exist.

I was so impressed with the new calculator, I couldn't wait to get my hands on it. Soon after returning from the convention, I had one in my hands. Out the door I went to make sales calls. Salespeople do think strange thoughts now and then, and I'm no exception. Every day on my way to work I drove on Interstate 10 and passed a sign on the side of the highway that had a cow on the top of it that rotated constantly. I always wanted to make a call on that cow, but could never find a reason—that is before now. I drove straight to that cow's building, electronic calculator in hand.

I entered the building and was directed to the purchasing department. When I opened the door of the purchasing department I fell into salesperson's heaven. The room was a chorus of chug-a-chug machines. There were twenty or more workers each with a chug-a-chug machine. I couldn't wait to show my calculator to the buyer. So I did. He almost had a heart attack when I multiplied *12 × 12* and *144* popped up in an instant. He couldn't believe his eyes. After I explained some of the very basic features of the machine, the buyer took it away from me and began punching in numbers. After a couple minutes playing with it, the buyer took a file from his desk and began entering numbers into one memory, then numbers into another memory. He multiplied one against the other then divided that answer by another number and said, "That's right!" To which I said, "What's right?" "The machine," he said.

The buyer went on to explain that all the employees in the other room were calculating the value of milk based on the quan-

tity as well as the butter fat content of the raw milk. He further
explained that the company chemist determined the butterfat
content of the raw milk farmers brought to this company, a dairy
processor. The department then calculated the amount to be paid
to the farmer using a formula based on the percentage of butter
fat in the milk. The buyer explained that the formula normally
took several minutes to calculate with the chug-a-chug machines
and could be solved in seconds with the electronic calculator. He
was impressed. After the buyer signed an order to purchase several calculators, I asked him to show me how the formula
worked. I was on cloud nine! I sold several machines the first
day. And these early calculators sold for approximately $3000
each.

Weeks and months went by until I received a call from my
regional sales manager. He wanted to know what was wrong. I
hadn't sold a single machine in three months, even though I was
the first to sell one after the convention. I shook my head and
said I didn't know what was wrong. "I'm making lots of calls," I
said, "I demonstrate the calculator several times every day. I'm
good with this machine. I just don't know why I'm not closing
sales."

Realizing my state of mind was low and knowing that I was
normally a top sales producer, my manager said he would come
to town the next week to work with me. Perhaps he could see
something I couldn't.

The manager arrived as scheduled the next week. To impress him, I made my first call the largest stock brokerage firm in
town. I wanted to impress upon my manager that I wasn't afraid
to call on anyone. After some resistance from the secretary, I managed to get in to see the person in charge. The presentation went
well, but once again I got the heave-ho with the old "we'll think
about it and get back to you" excuse.

After we left the building my manager looked at me and
said, "Good news! I've determined your problem." I said, "Great,
what is it?" He said, "Do you know what the buyer thought of
you after you completed your presentation?" "I think he liked
me," I said, "We got along well. I think he was impressed." "You

are absolutely right", my manager said, "In fact that fellow was so impressed with your knowledge and skill, that right now he is saying to himself that if he was just half as smart as you are he could probably operate that very complicated calculator." "What happened to twelve times twelve," he asked, "the way you were taught to demonstrate?"

The problem was that I was demonstrating the capability of this fine calculator by showing them how to calculate butter fat content with the complicated formula I learned during my first sale. I was attempting to show my prospects the enormous potential of my calculator. I was so good with the calculator that I was a blur of activity, hitting keys, dividing, saving in both memories, and then multiplying one against the other. The prospect was lost two seconds into the presentation. It was at that moment I remembered Ira Hayes' words. "Keep it simple, stupid!" Keep it simple and smart!

Always keep it simple. Ask yourself what would be important to you if you were the customer. Then by all means explain the benefits of each feature you demonstrate to your prospect. Every time you explain a feature, ask yourself, "So what?" That will remind you to explain the *what*, the benefit to the prospect. Remember, sell the *feature*, then the *advantage* of the feature, and last, the *benefit* to the customer (FAB).

A sales presentation should be designed to build value. Besides solving the basic need, a customer needs to feel good about paying your price. If your product is worth the money, tell the prospect why it is. However, remember to keep it simple. Practice on your spouse, your children, or a friend. Ask them if they understand what you are saying and what you mean. Practice your presentation over and over until it is perfect. Practice, practice, practice and have the courage to practice some more.

Once you develop and perfect a presentation that sells benefits and solves problems, success will be automatic and intentional rather than accidental.

$$CI + PPA = SOP$$

Correct Image + Planned Positive Action = Success on Purpose

6

Closing the Sale

When telling a prospect about the investment required to purchase your product use the word *only*. "The investment for this product, Mr. Prospect, is only $2995." If you believe it's a good buy, show it with your enthusiasm. If you believe your price is too high, it is, and the customer will feel that way too. Notice that I used *investment*, not *price*. Tom Hopkins in his books and videotapes explains negative and positive words, words to avoid and words to use in their place. *Investment* is a better word than *price*. *Investment* means that I could get a return on my money. *Price* is the same as *cost*. If it costs me money I don't want it. No one wants to buy; everyone wants to own.

Read Tom Hopkins book *How to Master the Art of Selling* and take a lesson from a master in the selling field. Watch television commercials closely. Notice how they build value while they make the investment a better value. Watch how they produce a sense of urgency to act now and save. Your presentation should do the same. A presentation to be most effective must build value and, more important, produce a sense of urgency. We all want many things we consider of value that we have not bought or may never buy. However, when we consider the purchase to be of urgent need, we buy *now*. Once you have completed the investment step, assume prospects will buy and ask them for the order.

Did You Know?

60 percent of potential buyers say *no* five times before they say *yes*

However

44 percent of salespeople stop asking for the order after the first *no*

22 percent of salespeople stop asking after the second *no*

14 percent of salespeople stop asking after the third *no*

12 percent of salespeople stop asking after the fourth *no*

92 percent of salespeople stop asking for the order before the fifth *no*

Conclusion

8 percent of salespeople close 60 percent of sales by asking the fifth time

In sales, you get what you expect. If you expect the prospect to shop around and if you believe that he or she will not buy now, that's what you will get (most of the time). On the other hand, if you expect the prospect to buy today, right now, and from you, that's what will happen (most of the time). It is critical that you go into every selling opportunity with the clear goal that you expect to leave with a signed order at the end of the presentation.

Read *Psycho-Cybernetics* by Dr. Maxwell Maltz. *Psycho-Cybernetics* clearly and scientifically explains why you are what you believe you are. The book also makes it clear why if you believe you will fail, you will. In the book, Maltz states, "One cannot act in conflict with one's own self image." He also says that, "Whatever the mind of man can conceive and believe, it can achieve."

To close a sale at the first appointment you have to be prepared. Your presentation has to be the best it can be. You must understand and believe that when prospects say *no*, they probably mean *know*. They just don't know *why* or if they should buy from you. They don't know why they should buy now.

THE CRYSTAL BALL ANALOGY

Do you own a crystal ball? Do any of your prospects own one? I don't. If your prospects did and they looked into it and saw that the night after your presentation a fire or burglary was going to happen in their home, would they want to take a few days to think about purchasing your system, or would they buy it immediately and insist that you install it tomorrow? Could they have a burglary or fire tomorrow? Sure, they could. Can you or I or anyone else guarantee it is not going to happen? Of course not. We have to develop a sense of urgency within prospects to motivate them to protect themselves now.

The first step toward closing sales is to believe in what you are selling. We must to close ourselves on the sale. We are often our own worst enemies. We must convince ourselves to expect sales now. Do you believe your company is good? Do you believe you are worth the money you charge? Do you believe the customer would be better off with your product than with your competitor's product? If your answer is *yes*, then you should try to persuade the prospect to buy from you now. Before we can make or ever expect the prospect to believe in us, we must first believe in ourselves.

Second, develop a sales presentation that deals with common objections before they arise.

Third, establish a sense of urgency to buy now.

Fourth, demonstrate professionalism and focus on and crystalize some of the problems the system is designed to defend against. The presentation must sell benefits.

Fifth, build value. The system in prospects' minds must be worth what you are asking. It doesn't matter how much you believe it is worth. It only matters how much prospects believe it is worth.

If you do these things, you will close sales without ever appearing to close. The prospects will simply take the product away from you. I am often asked, when do you start closing? My answer is, as soon as you start talking. You should be closing all the time.

Of course, there will be times when your prospects won't take the product away from you, and you will have to close the sale. I'll list again the objections commonly heard from prospects and attempt to find answers to those objections.

- The prospect wants to shop around.
- The product costs more than expected.
- The prospect wants to think about it.
- The prospect does not trust the salesperson.
- The prospect does not perceive a need for the product.
- The prospect is afraid to make a bad decision.

WHAT IS A GOOD CLOSING PERCENTAGE?

You can't close every sale, and that's okay. Let's say I am a 33 percent closer. That means that I will make a sale, over a period of time, in one of three presentations. Isn't that right? Other than improving my percentages, I must accept the fact that two people of three will tell me *no*. That's the way it works. If, for example, I earn $300 on each sale, then

How much did I earn when I received the first *no*?
How much did I earn when I received the second *no*?
How much did I earn when I received the *yes*?

If you answered $100 for each question you are correct. If you are a one out of three closer, to receive one *yes*, it is required that you receive two *no*s. There is no other way. Of course, you can improve your closing ratio, but the rule still applies and only the percentage changes.

TYPES OF PURCHASES

There are two types of purchases—planned and emergency.

There are *planned purchases*. I plan to buy a refrigerator. I know how much I will spend, and I know when I want to buy it. I plan to buy clothing. I plan to buy furniture, a new microwave, a television, a stereo system. These purchases are planned events for which I may budget.

There are *emergency purchases*, unplanned expenses. It's the middle of summer and my home is hot. It should be cool. I put my hand over an air duct and warm air is coming out. Then I check the compressor and it isn't running. I call a service technician who puts a hand over the air duct and tells me warm air is coming out. I knew that. The technician then tells me I need a new compressor. I didn't plan to buy a new compressor, but now I have to buy one. I'm not going to be miserable all summer while I save enough money to buy a compressor. I'm going to find the money as soon as possible, now. While driving down the street my transmission falls out. I didn't plan to buy a transmission but I'm going to buy one. I need my car. These are emergency purchases.

What I have to do as a salesperson is make sure the prospect sees the purchase of my product as an emergency purchase rather than a planned purchase. I have to establish an emergency with regard to my product or service. Once the emergency exists, all the prospect has left to do is look for the money to purchase the product.

People don't like to buy under emergency conditions. They simply have to. When my car needed a new transmission, I didn't want to buy one, I had to. When the transmission dealer handed me the estimate I hated him and I hated his bill, but I had to buy the parts and service and so I did. People don't want to buy security. They hate the idea of having to spend money on a security system. They hate that the crime problem is so bad they have to protect themselves with an alarm system. However, they'll buy it because they need it.

The following chapter describes steps to the closing process that when used properly and practiced regularly will increase your closing percentage.

7

The Eight-Step Closing Pattern

THE FIRST STEP: LISTEN

This sounds like a terribly simple statement: Listen completely and intently. However, salespeople and people in general can be terrible listeners. We tend to want to speak before the prospect is finished talking. As soon as we hear the first few words come out of the prospect's mouth, we think we know what they are going to say and we tune them out. We begin formulating our answer. When we do that, however, we no longer hear what the prospect is saying. The prospect sounds like the teacher in the Charlie Brown movies. All we hear is noise.

Instead of listening we begin to formulate our response to the objection. We are thinking that as soon as the prospect's mouth stops moving, we are going to say this and that. The problem with tuning out prospects is that we don't hear all they have to say. Or we don't completely understand what they mean by what they are saying.

There is a story about a five-year-old boy playing with a neighbor child.

> He came running into his house and ran up to his mother and asked, "Mommy, mommy, where did I come from? His mother took a deep breath. She had prepared for the day her son would finally ask this age-old question. However, she thought he would be older before this question surfaced. She sat her son down, got out some books, and began explaining reproduction. She explained how two people fall in love and marry. How the mother produces an egg, the father's sperm fertilizes the egg, and the egg becomes an embryo and then a child. When she was finished she breathed a sign of relief that she had gotten through it. She then asked her son if the explanation answered his question. With a somewhat puzzled look on his face he looked up to her and said, "I guess so, it's just that Billy next door said he came from Cleveland."

The little boy's mother thought she heard and understood the question so she tuned out, thought about what she was going to say, and then answered. She answered the wrong question. Listen completely and carefully. Make certain you understand the objection.

THE SECOND STEP: PAUSE AND THINK ABOUT WHAT WAS SAID

Did my son want to know the facts of life? Or was he asking a geography question? Sometimes while you're pausing (thinking about it), prospects change the objection or decide upon hearing themselves object that the objection was not valid. Simply by pausing for a few seconds and carefully thinking about what your prospect said, you may close the sale with your silence. Have you heard the saying "silence is golden"? In selling, and at this point, it truly is.

THE THIRD STEP: EMPATHIZE

To make it easier for you to overcome so-called objections, you must learn to use a cushion of understanding (empathy) when handling the objection. Empathy acts as a bridge or cushion for you to use to get in step with your prospect before attempting to overcome the objection.

When you use the bridge or cushion of understanding you are not necessarily agreeing with your prospect. As a ridiculous example, we'll suppose the prospect uses the objection that your company is a bunch of crooks. You could not afford to say, "You are certainly right." On the other hand, if you answer, "You are wrong," you have hit the prospect's objection head on, and a mental wall has been built between you and your prospect. When this happens you are inviting trouble and making the objection much harder to overcome. When you use empathy you ease prospects onto a big, soft cushion. When they are relaxed you answer.

Empathy is putting yourself into the shoes or skin of your prospects and seeing things through their eyes or from their point of view. When you do this, you are stepping to their side, lessening the likelihood of an argument. You and the prospects are getting in step so you can overcome the objection.

Take for example a prospect who says, "I have a friend in the business and I have to buy from her." The first thing you do is use a big, soft cushion of empathy. Ask yourself, "How would I feel if I were in this prospect's shoes?" If I had a friend in the business, I certainly would want to give him some business, provided it doesn't cost me. Now, you have the thinking of the prospect in mind.

You now know how to word the cushion of empathy to get in step with the prospect. You say something like this, "I understand how you feel. If I had a friend in the business I certainly would want to give him some of my business." You haven't told the prospects you agree with them, you have just let them know you understand how they feel. Once this has been accomplished, the prospect's resistance to your overcoming the objection has been lowered greatly.

If you're having trouble overcoming objections, chances are you're excited about what you are selling and you dive right into answering the objection before using a big, soft cushion of understanding and empathy. The professional salesperson has a number of good empathy cushions for use in any sales presentation to make the sales presentation sparkle. If you have only one and use it over and over, it becomes boring to prospects. Later in this chapter, you will be given a number of empathy and understanding cushions to use before you attempt to answer your prospects' objections. These examples can be built upon to suit your own personality.

THE FOURTH STEP: REPEAT BUT CHANGE THE OBJECTION

Let's suppose the prospect's objection is, "The price is too high, I don't think I can afford it." The repeat but change step should be as follows, "Just to clarify my thinking, what you are saying is that you would like to own a [blank] and you would purchase it as soon as possible, but you are not sure how your budget will accommodate the investment. Is that about right?"

Do you see how I changed the objection? I changed the objection to an objection I would prefer to hear. However, I ended the change by repeating what was said. Of course, we would all prefer to hear prospects say that they want our product just as soon as possible. Ninety nine times out of one hundred, when you repeat the objection in this manner, the prospect will answer yes.

THE FIFTH STEP: ISOLATE THE OBJECTION

Before answering the objection, make sure this is the only objection. If you skip this step, you take the risk that while you answer the first objection, the prospect is thinking of another to throw at you when you finish talking. To avoid this problem, say to the prospect, "Other than the investment figure, is there anything else that would keep you from saying 'let's put the product in right away'?"

If the prospects have other objections, get them to tell you now. If they have another objection, isolate that one also. If there are no other objections, proceed to the next step.

Remember, people lie. We like to believe we are all honest, but we all lie, withhold, or stretch the truth occasionally. Have you ever heard the saying "buyers are liars"? Sure! We all say things we don't mean. Let me show you how true this is.

I'm like most if not all men. What do you think I was thinking when I first asked my wife to dance on the first day I met her? It wasn't, "I want to spend the next 25 years living with you." It wasn't, "I want to pay all the bills for the rest of my life." It wasn't, "I want to have dinner with you or have a drink." I simply disguised it as all those things. I simply walked up her and began "shooting the bull." I told her a lot of things that had nothing to do with what was really on my mind. This, my friends, is called the *demo*. Meanwhile, all the time I knew my goal. I knew where I was going, and I have a suspicion she knew where I was heading. It's all part of the game called love.

Next, we're dating and I am heading toward the close. I've done all I can do to get to this point. I put my arm around her and go for a trial close. Then *rap*, she hits me! Do I stop? Do I leave and say, okay I give up? No way! I just retreat a few steps and start over. That's the way the game is played. We all sell, ask for agreement, and close in everyday life. Nothing happens until a sale is made. Sales aren't made very often if we don't have the conviction and mental fortitude to ask for the order.

In case you are wondering, my wife and I both won the game. Debbie and I have been married for twenty-seven wonderful years. I wonder who closed whom?

THE SIXTH STEP: ANSWER THE OBJECTION

Answer the objection with one of the following:

1.   An oral answer
2.   The written word
3.   An answer from a third party

As I travel the country working with sales organizations, I always ask my audience to share with me the type of objections they hear in their particular field of selling. It never ceases to amaze me how similar the objections are. It doesn't seem to matter what one sells, the top three objections are usually the following:

I want to think it over.

We plan to shop around.

The price is too high.

Regardless of the type of objections you usually hear in your field of sales, doesn't it make sense to list the top three at the very least and find and rehearse the answers to the top three? I think so. But the fact is that most salespeople haven't done this and are therefore not prepared to handle the most common objections they will face in everyday selling situations. This fact perhaps explains the old 80/20 rule. Eighty percent of sales are made by twenty percent of salespeople. I suspect it's the twenty percent who know and practice the answers to at least the top three objections they will hear. In the pages that follow, I give examples of closes to the most common objections and how these closes are used.

THE SEVENTH STEP: QUALIFY— THAT SOLVES THAT, DOESN'T IT?

The *qualify* step (called the *confirmation* step by some salespeople) allows the prospect the opportunity to agree with the case you've made in the answer. Agreement by the prospect does not mean having to say *yes*. All that is necessary is a sound, shrug, blink, or anything else other than *no*. Anything else is a *yes*. Timing is important here. When you make the qualifying statement, pause only briefly and wait for the nod, shrug, or other sign and then move quickly and confidently to the next step.

THE EIGHTH STEP: ASK FOR THE ORDER

Example: "Would an installation on Tuesday or Wednesday be better?" With your head down and pen poised in hand, be ready to write the answer on the order form. Remember, the next one who speaks buys. Too many salespeople buy their own products back at this point by opening their mouths. Silence is golden.

EXAMPLES OF CUSHION OF EMPATHY

PROSPECT: I don't make snap decisions. I always think about purchases overnight before I decide. I've been burned before.

SALES CONSULTANT: I don't blame you at all, if that happened to me, I would feel the same way.

PROSPECT: I want to be sure that I'm getting the best price and deal.

SALES CONSULTANT: I can understand how you feel. We are all looking for ways to save money, and if it will save you money in the long run, I'm all for it.

PROSPECT: We planned on seeing lots of companies to find out what's available.

SALES CONSULTANT: I can understand that. Many people feel that way at first because this is not an item you buy every day. It's natural for you to want to know more about it.

PROSPECT: We can't afford that much.

SALES CONSULTANT: Jack, I certainly can put myself in your shoes. I know what it takes to rear a family today.

PROSPECT: I really want to think this over. I'll tell you what, we'll get back with you in a couple of weeks.

SALES CONSULTANT: Jane, when you say you want to think it over, I know just how you feel. My wife and I usually do the same thing.

PROSPECT: I really don't think we need an alarm system.

SALES CONSULTANT: Jack, I can understand that. Can I talk to you as if you were my brother?

PROSPECT: We have insurance. Frankly we would be better off if they stole some of this old stuff we have.

SALES CONSULTANT: I can understand that. Jane, there is something important I'd like to say, but I wouldn't want you angry with me. May I say it?

PROSPECT: There is nothing in this house worth protecting.

SALES CONSULTANT: Jack, no matter what you might say [say it with a big smile], you'll never persuade me you're anything but a nice guy [good husband, good father]. Because all I have to do is look around your home and see the many fine things you have provided for your family.

8

Answering the Objections

When answering an objection, you must first restate the objection.

Benefits to You

1. Restating the objection gives you the opportunity to find out if you really understand your prospect's objection.
2. By restating the objection you have the opportunity to rephrase it and an opportunity to add your own words to strengthen your position.

PROSPECT: I can't afford it.

[Pause]

SALES CONSULTANT'S EMPATHETIC ANSWER: Certainly no one knows your financial position better than you do, Mrs. Jones.

However, just to clarify my thinking, in other words, you do want a [your product or service], but the question in your mind is it may not fit into your budget at the present time. Does that seem to be your concern?

[Wait for the answer]

CONSULTANT: I can easily put myself in your shoes. I wasn't born with a silver spoon in my mouth. I've had to work hard for every dollar I've ever earned. Here's something I know will interest you. There are basically two types of purchases—the planned type, such as clothing and cars, and emergency or unplanned purchases. A [your product] usually is an unplanned or emergency purchase. We purchase an alarm system to protect our families against a possible tragedy. It's unplanned because we don't want to install one; we do so because we don't want to become victims and because we don't know when tragedy will strike. Isn't that so?

We at Action Alarm Company have a plan that works well for all of us very normal people who occasionally need help with finances. Our plan allows you to enjoy the benefits of an XYZ system with only a modest ten percent initial investment followed by small monthly installments. That handles that problem, doesn't it?

[Pause]

Which day would be better for your installation, Thursday or Friday?

The next one who speaks buys.

QUALIFY: GET AGREEMENT

The *get agreement* step follows the *answer* step in the closing pattern. It does just what it implies. It gets agreement from prospects that your answer has fully satisfied any question or so-called objections that had been on their minds. When you get this agreement, you have every right to ask for the order.

Examples of Qualifying Questions

Don't you agree?

That makes sense, doesn't it?

Can you see my point?

Isn't that so?

Isn't that right?

Isn't that the way you want to feel?

Isn't that terrific?

9

Twelve Powerful Closes

There are only a few objections you will hear over and over again. The following are twelve powerful closes that have been industry tried and proved to answer those objections. Memorize them. Practice them until the words flow smoothly and naturally. Don't skip any of the steps, and you will appear conversational rather than confrontational.

THE MANUFACTURER'S CHOICE CLOSE

This close is used to answer a price objection, especially when the difference in price is large. Here's how it goes:

> You know, Mr. Prospect, every manufacturer has a choice. They have the choice of producing the cheapest product knowing that the quality will not be as good. These manufacturers also realize that their customers are not the most demanding type and generally expect what they

get, which is low quality. This manufacturer also expects to sell this type of product in volume. A manufacturer also has the choice to produce only the best product it can, using the best parts, and employing the best people. These manufacturers recognize that they will make fewer sales but to more discriminating clients who expect and demand quality.

Because our business is protecting lives, my company made the choice to produce only the best. When it comes to life safety, only the best is good enough. Mr. and Mrs. Prospect, how do you want me to protect your family: The best way I can, using the best equipment and installation techniques or the cheapest way I can?

OUR BEST INSTALLER CLOSE

Everyone has a best installer. The best installer close works this way:

> Jack and Mary, now that you know about our system and the investment, the only thing we have to decide is whom we are going to trust in your home. We are fortunate to have the best installer in the industry working for us. His name is Jimmy. Jimmy gets letters from customers thanking him for the great job he has done. He is so good with our customers that some have said they would like to adopt him. Let me call the office and see when Jimmy is available next.

Immediately get up and start walking to the phone. Pick up the phone and dial the office, your home, the time, anyone. "Hello Sally, this is Lou. I'm at the Smith residence and I need an installation date for the Smiths using Jimmy's crew. When will they be available? Next Tuesday? Okay, hold on." Put your hand over the phone and say, "Jack and Mary, we can get Jimmy next Tuesday or Frank this Friday. I'd rather see Jimmy do this job. Will it be Jimmy next Tuesday or Frank this Friday?"

The next one who speaks buys.

THE INSURANCE CLOSE

Objection "I've never experienced a burglary and I've lived in this house twenty years."

Listen

Pause

Empathize "I certainly can understand how you feel, I wouldn't want to spend money on something I didn't need!"

Repeat but change "Just to clear up my thinking, what you're saying is you like this system and would have it installed as soon as possible, but since you've never experienced a burglary, you don't see the need. Is that about right?"

"That's it," the prospect says.

Isolate "Other than need, is there anything else that would keep you from having the system installed right away?"

"No, we've never had a problem here."

Answer "Well, I can certainly understand that. Let me ask you a question. Do you know, off hand, what your annual home-owner's insurance premium is?"

"Yes, it's eight hundred dollars."

"Eight hundred dollars, I see. Have you ever had a fire?"

"No."

"That's great. Insurance for your home in the event of a fire is still a good investment. We all should have good insurance. How long have you lived in this home?"

"Twenty years."

"And how long do you expect to continue to live here?"

"Oh, until the kids are on their own and we retire. I suppose another ten years."

"I see, so if we add the twenty years you've already lived here to the ten you plan to stay, we have a total of thirty years. Now if we multiply thirty years by the eight hundred dollar insurance premium, we find that you have or will have invested $24,000 in homeowners insurance. Here's a drawing of your house. [Draw a box with a roof on it. Draw a line down through the roof through the middle of the house and say the following.]

"You see you have or will have invested $24,000 to protect half your house. Insurance protects the walls, ceiling, roof, the structure, along with the furnishings and fixtures. What I'm asking you to do is to invest only $2,500 to protect the other half of your home—you, your spouse, and the kids."

Qualify Family is the most important part of a home, isn't it? [It's not necessary for the prospects to say yes, anything except an absolute *no* is a *yes* in my book.]

Ask for the order "Will Tuesday or Thursday be best for installation?"

The next one who speaks buys.

THE REFRIGERATOR CLOSE

Objection "I don't think I need a system enough to spend $2,500."

Listen

Pause

Empathize I can understand how you feel. I wasn't born with a silver spoon in my mouth either. I wouldn't want to spend money on something I didn't need.

Repeat but change "Just to clarify my thinking, what you're saying is that you really like this system and would have it installed as soon as possible if you needed it enough to invest $2,500. Is that about right?"

"Yes."

Isolate "Other than need, is there anything else that would keep you from saying, 'Hey, Lou, let's get this system installed right away?'"

"No, if I needed it, I'd buy it."

Answer   "Sure, I can understand that. [Pause while looking at their refrigerator.]

"What make of refrigerator is that?"

"Amana."

"Do you recall how much you paid for it?"

"Oh, about nine hundred dollars."

"Nine hundred dollars. If you took all the food out of the refrigerator and totaled the value of it all, how much do you suppose it would all be worth?"

"I'd say about seventy dollars."

"Seventy dollars. I'd guess that's about the average value of food in almost anyone's refrigerator. You see, you have invested nine hundred dollars to protect approximately seventy dollars worth of food. What I'm asking you to do is invest $2,500 to protect yourself, your family, the house and everything in it, including that refrigerator and the food in it."

Qualify   "That make sense, doesn't it?"

Ask for the order   "So, would Monday or Friday be better for the installation?"

The next one who speaks buys.

THE PARACHUTE CLOSE

Objection   "How much is the system, $2,500? I thought it would cost $395. I didn't want to spend that much."

Listen

Pause

Empathize   "I can truly understand how you feel. I'm a family man myself. I know how hard it is to rear a family in these trying times."

Repeat but change   "Let me see if I understand what you're saying. You really like the system and would have us install it as soon as possible, but you think it costs too much. Is that right?"

"Sure."

Isolate   "Other than the cost of the system, is there anything else that would keep you from saying, 'Hey Lou, let's get my family protected right away?'"

"No, that's it."

"I understand. Let's see if we can put this in perspective. Let's assume for a moment that you and your spouse have won an all- expenses-paid trip for two to Europe. Let's say today is the day you're leaving and the two of you are on a 747 airplane that just took off from Kennedy Airport.

"A few minutes later the pilot clicks on the microphone and you expect to hear the announcement that the plane is leveling off to a cruising altitude of 30,000 feet. However, this is what you hear:

> Ladies and gentlemen, this is your pilot speaking. I'm afraid I have some bad news for you. It seems that we have lost power in all four engines. We've done all we can to jump start them to no avail. I'm afraid the plane is going down. Further bad news is that the ground crew apparently failed to put passenger parachutes on board, so good luck.

"Just about then, Mr. and Mrs. Jones, you look out the window and see four parachutes floating down to safety. You and the other passengers are doomed.

"When all seems lost, I introduce myself to you as a parachute salesman. I say:

> You're in luck. I happen to be a parachute salesman, and I have several parachutes with me, enough to get everyone off the plane. Now, I have two types of parachutes for you to choose from. The first is the economy model. It sells for $395 and is guaranteed to open most of the time.

However, it does come with a money back guarantee. If it doesn't open, send it on back to us and we'll give you your money back. We also have the deluxe model parachute guaranteed to open all the time. It sells for $2500.

"Let me ask you a question. Which parachute would you strap on your back?"
"The $2500.00 one."
"Of course, when it comes to your life, money is unimportant."

Qualify   "Isn't that so?"

Ask for the order   "What day would be best to provide that life-saving protection? Wednesday? Or would Thursday be better?"

THE REDUCE TO THE RIDICULOUS CLOSE

Objection   "The price is too high, five hundred dollars too much. The system costs more than I expected."

Listen

Pause

Empathize   "I can understand how you feel. I've had to work hard for my money. I surely wouldn't want to spend too much for anything."

Repeat but change   "Just to clarify my thinking, what you are saying is that you like the system and would have it installed right away, but it cost too much. Is that your concern?"
"That's it. Lower the price enough and we've got a deal."

Isolate   "Other than price, is there anything else standing in the way of protecting your family?"
"No, that's it."
"I see. May I ask how much too high the price is?"

"About five hundred dollars."

"I see. So if we could reduce the investment for our system by five hundred dollars, you'd say let's do it?"

"Yes, I would."

"Unfortunately we can't do that. Our system is worth what we ask, but let's see if we can put this in perspective."

"Would you agree that this system should be effective for you for at least ten years?

"Yes, I expect so."

"If we divide the five hundred dollar difference by ten years, we're talking only fifty dollars per year, approximately four dollars per month, one dollar a week. We're talking about investing approximately fourteen cents per day to have the absolutely best system to protect you, your family, and your children."

Qualify   "Surely that's a small investment to make, isn't it?"

Ask for the order   "Will Tuesday or Thursday be best for the installation?"

THE SHOPPING AROUND CLOSE

Objection   We'll make the decision after we see the other two companies."

Listen

Pause

Empathize   "I can certainly understand that. The decision to protect my family would be something worth investigating."

Repeat but change   "Just to clear up my thinking, what you're saying is that you like our system and would have it installed as soon as possible, but when it comes to protecting your family, you want to be sure that you select the very best. Is that about right?"

"That's right."

Isolate   "Other than your desire to look at two other companies, is there anything else that would prevent you from giving me the go ahead tonight?"

"No, I like your system. After I see the other companies, if it's still the best system, you'll get the order."

Answer   "That's great! One thing is certain, the harder you look around at other systems, the better my system will look. When do you expect to see the next company?"

"Next week on Friday."

"Okay, so that's six days from today. When do you plan to see the third company?"

"We have an appointment for the Friday after that."

"So, that's about two weeks from today. Okay. Because I don't have the gift of prophecy, as I'm sure you don't — and because we don't, we can't be sure a burglary or worse, a fire, won't happen in the meantime, here's what we'll do for you. Because we are so confident about our product and because we would like to see your family protected, we'll send a crew to your home tomorrow morning and install the system. [Take out the ACME Alarms Fourteen Day Free Trial certificate and say]:

> As this fourteen-day certificate guarantees, take the next two weeks and look at other systems. If after shopping around you find a better system for the protection of your family, one you'd rather have, give us a call and we'll promptly remove our system. Worse case is that you will benefit from two weeks of free protection while you looked around. Best case is you'll confirm for yourself what I've said today, and you have been protected all along.

Qualify   "That makes sense, doesn't it?"

Ask for the order   "Will eight in the morning be good, or would nine be better?"

The next one who speaks buys.

THE BEN FRANKLIN CLOSE

Objection "We'll need time to think this over."

Listen

Pause

Empathize "I can understand that. A decision as important as protecting your family is one that requires thought."

Repeat but change "Let me see if I completely understand you. What you're saying is you really like our system and would like to have it installed as soon as possible, but you want to be sure you're making the right decision. Is that right?"
"Yes."

Isolate "Other than not being sure and needing time to think this over, is there anything else that is preventing you from proceeding with the protection?"
"No, that's all."

Answer "I'm sure you've heard of Ben Franklin. Well, Ben had a reputation as being a great decision maker. One day people he knew approached Ben and asked him how he was able to make such good decisions. Ben said:

> It's quite simple. Anytime I'm faced with a difficult decision, I get out a piece of paper. I draw a line across the top and then down the middle. On the left side of the center line I write down all the reasons I should do what I'm considering. After I run out of reasons why I should, on the other side of the line I write down the reasons I shouldn't. When I'm finished, I simply count the reasons in the columns and put the answer at the bottom. If there are more reasons why I should do what I was thinking about, I do it. If there are more reasons why I should not do it, I don't. It's that simple.

"So, Mr. and Mrs. Jones, why don't we try that method. Let's start with the reasons we should install the system." [Note: The sale consultant should have a list of ten or more benefits prospects will agree they will receive when protected with the system. The following are examples:

The system would provide peace of mind, would it not?

You'd feel more comfortable at night while asleep?

Your children would be safer at home after school before the
　　first adult arrives home, right?

After listing the benefits, it's time to list the reasons not to buy the system. This time don't help the prospects.

"Now, why don't we list the reasons why we shouldn't protect your family." [Don't say a word, let the prospects talk. Whatever they say, respond as follows.]

"Okay, that's [two] reasons."

Rarely will prospects come up with more than two *no*s. Wrap up the close by saying:

"Now let's see what we have here. We have ten reasons why we should say yes and we have only two reasons for saying no. Old Ben Franklin would say the answer is simple, *yes* wins."

Qualify　"That makes good sense doesn't it?"

Ask for the order　"Would Monday be a good day to start, or would Thursday be better?"

THE TAKE IT AWAY CLOSE

This close requires preparation. While presenting your product, you must demonstrate features of your company, system, design, or anything that is unique or special. It's necessary to get acknowledgment from the prospects that the demonstrated features are important to them.

Objection   "The price you're asking is too high."

Listen

Pause

Empathize   "I can understand how you could feel that way. No one wants to spend too much for anything."

Repeat but change   "To make sure I fully understand you, you're saying that you really like this system and you'd like to have it as soon as possible, but you feel it costs a bit too much. Is that how you feel?"

"Sure, that's it!"

Isolate   "Other than the cost's being too high, is there anything else that would prevent you from saying, 'Hey Lou, let's get that system in and my family protected as soon as possible?'"

"No, it's that the price is high."

Answer   "Great! Let me ask you, how much too high is it?"

"Oh, about five hundred dollars."

"In other words, if we could lower the cost by five hundred dollars you'd say let's get it installed?"

"Yep!"

"Great! Let's see what we can do. Remember the talking feature I showed you that would notify you and the family in a clear voice if your home were on fire? I remember you really liked it. We could eliminate it and save you $250. Would you like me to take that feature away?"

"Oh, no. I like that feature. I wouldn't want to give it up."

"I see. So, aren't you saying that my system is worth $250 more?"

"I guess so."

"Of course. So then I guess we are only $250 apart aren't we?"

"That's right."

"Now there was another special feature of our system that we could take out, the telephone-arming, panic feature. By taking that away, we could save another $210. Would you like me to take it away?"

"No, I like that feature as well."

"Then, of course, our system is worth the $210 more, and we are only $40 apart."

Qualify   "There are other features we could take out, but it seems clear that this system is the right one for you, isn't it?"

Ask for the order   "Would Tuesday or Thursday be best to start the protection?"

The next one who speaks, buys.

THE COLUMBO CLOSE

Sometimes after you attempt several closes to no avail, the Columbo close is a great "on the way out the door" close. One of the keys to this close is to pack up your brief case and demo kit and start to leave. However, as Detective Columbo would do, stop at the door and ask the following question:

> Mr. and Mrs. Prospect, can I ask a favor of you? Tomorrow morning, when I go to my office, my manager will ask me if I protected your home. When I tell him no, he's going to ask me why not. Could you help me out? I'm not sure what to say. Can you tell me why I wasn't able to persuade you that our system is the best?

Often, when you ask this question in this way and at this time, prospects tell you the real objection—the one they've been holding back all night. Once they tell you, you're back into the closing steps:

Listen

Pause

Empathize

Repeat but change

Isolate

Answer

Qualify

Ask for the order

ASSUMPTIVE CLOSE

This is the first close we should always use. Simply put, assume that prospects have bought, and ask for their okay on the agreement (not *contract*). If your prospects have not actually said they do not want to buy, assume they do want to buy. If you act as if prospects are not prepared to make a decision, they sense your insecurity and stall.

IMPENDING EVENT CLOSE

This close produces a sense of urgency to buy now because the burglars will come back, the price is going up, the crews are getting busy, or there is a special promotion they should take advantage of now. Department stores use an impending close every month. There are the going back to school sales, close-out sales, before Christmas sales, and after Christmas sales. They establish a sense of urgency in us to make us feel that if we don't run down to the store and buy now, the product will be gone or cost more tomorrow. The impending event close gives us the push we need to make a decision.

It's been said that we are motivated to buy on the basis of one of three factors—desire, need, or greed. An impending event type of close addresses all three reasons.

Qualify: Get Agreement   The get agreement step follows the answer step in the closing pattern. It does what it implies. It gets agreement from prospects that your answer has fully satisfied any question or so-called objection that on their minds. When you get this agreement, you have every right to ask for the order.

Examples of Qualifying Questions

Don't you agree?

That makes good sense, doesn't it?

Can you see my point?

Isn't that so?

Isn't that right?

Isn't that the way you want to feel?

Isn't that terrific?

10

The Power of Role Playing

In every sales and closing seminar I conduct, an appreciable amount of time is devoted to role playing. I divide participants into teams of two each, and they take turns playing the salesperson's role and the customer's role. After some practice, I videotape the role-playing sessions for playback. The first reaction of the class to videotaped role playing is one of fear and apprehension. However, the evaluations I receive after the class prove that role playing is enjoyable and useful. There is nothing I can think of that will improve one's selling skills more than role playing. However, it is important that the role playing is conducted correctly. I'm sure we have all heard the saying "practice makes perfect." But the fact is only perfect practice makes perfect.

MENTAL PRACTICE

A classroom environment is an excellent place to practice role-playing techniques. You can also practice role playing during a regularly scheduled sales meeting. However, inasmuch as role playing so greatly affects our success, it is in our own best interest to (perfectly) practice as much as possible.

During my days with NCR Corporation, Frank Leon, my sales manager, would turn off the radio in my car every time he rode with me during the business day on sales calls. His feeling was that the radio was a distraction I could do without. Instead, Frank would say, "Think about the call you are going to. Think about what you will say when you arrive. Imagine what the prospect will say in response and what you will say in response to the response. Rehearse the call from start to successful finish. It is a better use of the time between calls." After a few rides with Frank in my car, I got into the habit of turning the radio off during the day as he suggested, and I began role playing my next call. Frank was absolutely right, and my sales improved as a result.

Frank shared that advice with me in 1970, two years after the first printing of *Psycho-Cybernetics* by Maxwell Maltz. *Psycho-Cybernetics* mentions much about the subject of mental role playing. Maltz asks the question, "Why not imagine yourself successful?" He then explains how mental pictures offer us an opportunity to practice new traits and attitudes that otherwise we would not have. This is possible because your nervous system and brain cannot tell the difference between a real or an imagined experience.

Maltz goes on to give examples of how mental role playing has been successfully used in improving skills in dart throwing, golf, chess, and other games. The most interesting example to me was the basketball experiment reported in *Research Quarterly* on the effects of mental practice in improving skills of sinking basketball free throws. In the experiment, students were divided into three groups. The first group's accuracy at the free throw line was measured on the first day. For the next twenty days the students practiced twenty minutes a day. Their accuracy was measured again on the twentieth day. The second group's accuracy also was measured, but the students were told not to practice. Twenty days later their accuracy was checked. The accuracy of the third group was measured on the first and the last day of the twenty-day test. These students, however, were asked to practice mentally but not physically shooting free throws twenty minutes a day every day and to do so for twenty consecutive days. The results of the test were as follows.

Group one, who practiced every day for twenty days improved in scoring by 24 percent. Group two, who hadn't practiced at all, showed no sign of improvement. Group three, who only imagined they were shooting free throws twenty minutes each day for twenty days, improved 23 percent—only 1 percent less than group one, who physically practiced for the full twenty days.

Similar studies were conducted with dart throwers, golfers, and chess players. In fact, a 1955 *Readers Digest* story told of a rather obscure chess player who challenged a champion chess player, who had never lost a match. The challenger trained for the match by going to the country, where he stopped smoking and drinking. He did calisthenics and for three months played chess only in his mind. The challenger, Akekhine, won the match, defeating the then undefeated champion, the great Capablanca.

Without question, role playing will polish selling skills to an all-time brilliant luster. What exactly is role playing? Role playing is enacting in your mind situations in selling in which you will find yourself involved. You can mentally visualize making cold calls and visualize what you will say when you enter the home. Think of what the prospect might say in response and about what your response will be. As you improve your visualization skills, you will be able to conduct entire presentations in your mind. The benefit to you is that when you are finally in front of prospects, you have practiced what you and they might say, and you are prepared.

Almost every type of game, such as football, basketball, bowling, billiards, and golf, involves mental practice or *visualization*, as it's more commonly known today, to improve ability and scores. I recently read an article in a sailing magazine that suggested that to improve their sailboat racing skills, sailors should visualize the race and everything they will be called upon to do in the race. By doing this, they dramatically improve their position at the finish line on race day.

If you follow the steps outlined in this book and have the patience and fortitude to practice, practice, and practice some more and if you will visualize successful selling on the way to and from sales appointments as well as during every spare moment you have, you will realize your goals. You will be a successful salesperson on purpose.

CI + PPA = SOP

Correct Image + Planned Positive Action = Success on Purpose

11

Why Do I Place So Much Emphasis on Closing?

Twenty years ago I answered an advertisement in the local newspaper for a sales management position with an alarm franchise operation in the New Orleans area. The director of marketing conducted the interview and two interviews later I was hired.

The day I started work, the owner of the franchise, a local attorney, directed me to the offices across town and said, "Go to work." I didn't receive even basic training. In fact, I had to introduce myself to the employees. After getting settled into my office and reading everything about the company and the products I could find around the office, I still didn't feel comfortable making a call. To fill in the blanks in my mind, and to get a better feel for alarm systems, I started calling existing customers.

I had a list of questions prepared to ask each customer I called. My goal was to find out why the customers purchased an alarm and, for my information, if buyer's remorse existed in the alarm industry. The following are some of the questions I asked:

How long have you had our system?

What motivated you to buy it?

Why did you buy your alarm system from us?

Are you happy with your alarm system?

If you had to make the decision to purchase an alarm system today, would you do anything differently?

What did you think about the salesperson who sold the alarm system to you?

Have you been happy with our service?

Have you recommended or would you recommend our company to your friends and relatives?

If you call every customer of any company, you will find at least one unhappy customer, and I fully expected to find one or more when I made my calls. Much to my surprise, almost everyone I called was happy, would buy again, and would buy from us. I didn't discover any buyer's remorse. I found some customers who wanted additional sensors and that was great, because, of course, I could sell them the additional sensors. I learned that most customers bought their systems after a problem had occurred in their neighborhood, their home, or at a friend or relative's home. I should mention that at the time, the company for whom I worked sold mostly fire alarm systems. In the early 1970s, most people did not see the need for burglar alarm systems.

After many calls, I was speaking with a woman who had positive comments about everything until I asked:

"What did you think about the salesperson?"

She answered, "You want to know what I thought of the salesman? I'll tell you what I thought." On the basis of the tone of her voice, I just knew I had finally found the angry customer. So I lied. I said, "Yes, I would."

"You have a salesman by the name of Frank Clement," she said. "Well, he was the pushiest salesman I've ever met. He wouldn't take no for an answer. I kept telling him I wasn't interested in a fire alarm system. My husband told him we weren't interested in a fire alarm. However, he just kept on talking."

"I'm very sorry," I said. "These things happen occasionally, but I apologize if we upset you."

"I'm not finished yet," she said. "I finally got so tired of him not taking no for an answer that I just got up and went upstairs to bed. I left my husband and your salesman downstairs. The next morning I asked my husband what happened, and he said that he bought the fire alarm system just to get rid of the salesman. He was convinced that Frank wouldn't leave otherwise."

Once again I jumped into the conversation and apologized for the pushy salesman. But once again she told me she was not finished yet:

This all happened just before the Christmas holidays. Every year, just before Christmas, we go to a neighbor's house for a little holiday get together, and this year was no exception. We leave our children, who were ten, twelve, and thirteen years old at the time, at home alone. We always felt okay leaving them alone at that age.

We had been at the party for about two and a half hours when we heard a commotion outside. We heard sirens. It became apparent that what we heard were fire trucks. We all scrambled outside. I looked down the street, and my heart jumped into my mouth. My house was on fire. With tears streaming down my face I ran toward my house. When I arrived, to my joy, my three kids and a firefighter were standing on the front lawn safe. The firefighter asked if I had installed a fire alarm system. I said I had. The fireman said, "It's a good thing you did because based on the speed with which the fire spread, without the early warning of a fire alarm system, your three kids would surely have died."

You want to know what I think of your salesman, Frank Clement? I owe my kids lives to Frank's belief and conviction that I needed a fire alarm system. I pray for and give thanks for Frank Clement every day of my life.

To this day, when I tell this story, tears form in my eyes. When I heard it the first time I was an emotional wreck. But more important, I learned early that fire alarms and burglar alarms are safety systems. They save lives. I also know I have to adhere to my beliefs and do everything within my power to persuade my prospects to install one today. Had Frank taken the easy road and stopped when he heard the first or second no, three children would have died. He didn't, and I don't either.

If you believe in your company and believe in your product, you owe it to your prospect and their families to close the sale today.

Things come to those who wait but only the things left behind by those who hustle!

12

Lead Generation: Prospecting

In the gold rush era, prospectors pored over the mountains of California in search of their fortune. Today's sales prospectors still do, but what they seek are leads. Leads are the life's blood of every salesperson and represent the difference between success and failure in the sales field. If you depend on call-ins to provide prospects for you, you most certainly will be relegated to mediocrity. If, however, you become self-sufficient, producing and working your own gold mine of fresh leads, your future and financial success are guaranteed.

WHAT IS PROSPECTING?

Gold miners looked for gold in two basic areas. Some dug into mountains in search of the mother lode, often difficult, unrewarding work. Other miners panned for gold in the streams running out of the mountains. Both looked for gold.

The panners sought to become rich a little at a time. The diggers sought to become rich on one big strike. In selling you can be either a digger or a panner depending on the product you sell. It is important to know which you're supposed to be. Residential and light commercial alarm sales is panning. A sale a day or at least one a week is required for success. Sales of heavy commercial, card-access systems, closed-circuit television system and industrial and high-rise fire alarm systems are digging.

Prospecting is the process of locating people potentially interested in the product you sell to set an appointment for a sales presentation. The goal of prospecting is to set appointments, not to sell the product. Tell a prospect only as much as it takes to make the appointment. You must avoid saying too much. There will be plenty of time for selling during the sales appointment. Prospecting is anything and everything you do to find people to whom to tell your story, to whom to make a presentation.

Nothing in the sales field has a more profound effect on your future than the ability to prospect effectively. At the beginning of this book, I told you what the sales guru said to me. He said, "One person of ten will buy anything you ask him or her to buy." If I prospect well, statistically I will make sales even if I'm a weak salesperson. Find a winner in the sales field and you have also found an excellent lead prospector.

Remember the 80/20 rule of sales? Eighty percent of sales are made by twenty percent of salespeople. I believe this is so largely because of prospecting habits. The sales champions (the twenty percent) know that prospecting is vital to their success. Therefore, they are constantly in search of new prospects and leave no stone unturned. Sales champions also employ more than one lead producer at a time, somewhat like dragging more than one fishing line behind a boat. The more you drag, the greater is your likelihood of eating.

The key to effective prospecting is diligence and persistence. Prospecting is not something you should do on a sporadic basis. Consistent effort pays in the long run. If you prospect continuously, you will be successful. If you do not, you won't; it's that simple.

People don't plan to fail, they simply fail to plan

The best way to ensure success is to plan to succeed. The success plan must be detailed and specific in its goals and aspirations. Lay out a specific attack plan regarding lead generation and then muster the courage to implement and adhere to the plan. Only quitters quit. Most losers are quitters, and most quitters are losers. Do you want to be a winner?

Prospecting is also an attitude. Prospecting can be easy and fun or difficult and painful. You control the results. If you approach prospecting with the mind-set that leads are there for you to find, that no one can hurt you but yourself, that the one of ten is waiting for you, then prospecting will become profitable and fun. However, you must start with a plan.

Plan your work, then work your plan

When I sold Kirby vacuum cleaners, daily prospecting was an absolute must. The most common prospecting method we used was the good old "belly to belly" method; we knocked on doors. Every day, at about ten in the morning, I selected a neighborhood I liked and I walked from door to door in search of three or more appointments for that day. My minimum goal was three because statistics said that one of three appointments could be canceled at the last minute, and my closing ratio was running close to fifty percent. Three appointments a day netted out to one sale a day, approximately one hundred dollars a day.

Kirby required all salespeople to attend the daily sales meeting held at about 8:30 in the morning. The goal of the meeting was to motivate us, to fire us up with enthusiasm. The managers knew that if we were enthusiastic and had the right mental attitude, we were in the best frame of mind to prospect. The morning meeting also included a volume report. The salespeople were asked what they sold the evening before. They were asked how they obtained the lead and how many closes they attempted before the order was signed. The design and intention of the meeting was to motivate us. And when it came to door-to-door canvassing, I needed motivation. Door-to-door canvassing never became easy for me. Every day I had to force myself out of the car to make the first call. However, after the first call was under my belt, canvassing became easier and actually fun. Finding an appointment became a challenge, one that produced tangible financial results.

> *Put me in a new city and after three sales I will never have a shortage of leads.*
>
> —Author unknown

13

Who Is a Prospect?

A prospect is anyone (1) who needs or will benefit from your product or service; (2) who can afford your product or services; and (3) who can attend a presentation of your product or service under favorable selling conditions, meaning all decision makers are present. All three conditions must be met.

To start your prospecting plan, sit down and ask yourself the following questions:

Who would benefit from my product and services? Make a list, by category, of people who meet the criteria.

What is the main benefit of each category?

Where or how can I locate these people? In priority order, which group shall I contact first?

LEAD SOURCES

Leads can be found in a number of different ways. It is important to restate that you should use varied sources at the same time. The most common lead sources are as follows:

Telemarketing
Direct mail
Bird dogs
Referrals
Cold calling
Business cards
Home shows
Neighborhood associations
Parent's clubs, Kiwanis, Rotary, and similar organizations
Customer visits
Tip clubs
Crime prevention officers and programs
Radio
Television
Newspaper
Coupons
Billboards, buses
School and church bulletins
Raffles, charity
Your company's vehicle
Flyers, door hangers
"Pardon our noise" door hangers during installations
Pass card lists
Those you know
Accounts payable lists
Repossessed house rental program
Use of outdated demonstration kits by rape victims
Yellow pages

There are twenty-eight sources in the list. If you implement them all, you won't have time to sell. So, implement two to three at first and then add additional programs gradually. Let's look at each one individually.

TELEMARKETING

Telemarketing can be broken down into three basic categories—personal telemarketing, use of in-house specialists, and contract telemarketing.

Personal Telemarketing

Personal telemarketing is simply a salesperson's making his or her own telemarketing calls. The effectiveness of personal tele-marketing calls depends on the following factors:

1. The number of calls made daily
2. The quality of the script used
3. The time of day the calls are made
4. The attitude of the caller
5. The quality of the list you use

If you call at random twenty-five people per day without a script and simply ask, "Are you interested in knowing more about my product?" and ask for an appointment, you can expect no more than one appointment for every 125 calls.

If you improve the script a bit through trial and error and call between 4 and 6 P.M., your results improve to about one and one half appointments for each one hundred calls.

If you make twenty-five telephone contacts per day using a good planned script, calling between 4 and 6 P.M., and targeting qualified buyers of your product, you can expect to set two to five appointments per one hundred calls.

So now you're asking, if this is so, why doesn't everyone do this? It's a good question. Personal telemarketing works, and the facts bare this truth out. Ask successful salespeople all over the country and they'll testify to the merits of telemarketing. Eighty percent of salespeople, however, won't consistently make the calls. Anyone want to guess why the 80/20 rule exists?

The problem is between the ears of the salesperson. How hard is it to make twenty-five phone calls? How much time can it take? What's the worst thing that could happen? Is it because salespeople dread rejection? They hate to hear the word *no*? They fear the hang-up?

It's all of the above. Salespeople want to be liked. They hate to be disliked. They believe that the prospect will be upset with them if they call and ask for an appointment. That is, eighty percent of salespeople feel that way. This is why the 80/20 rule exists.

Twenty percent of salespeople know that the prospect on the other end of the phone line can't hurt them. They expect rejection. They work the odds. They consider every *no* as a step closer to a *yes*. They work to perfect their phone skills to improve their call-to-appointment ratio. They know that the telephone is their friend, a friend that makes money for them. To be successful at telemarketing your own leads, you must do the following:

1. Develop a script that in a few words effectively conveys your message and asks for an appointment.
2. Determine who your prospect is and acquire a list of names and phone numbers that contains the type of prospect you want. List brokers sell specific types of lists for thirty to forty dollars per thousand names. Or you can drive the neighborhoods in which your prospect lives, noting street names and numbers. Then use a crisscross directory to find the phone numbers for the addresses you located.
3. Diligently call a minimum of twenty-five prospects every day of the week. Don't make excuses, do it.
4. Call between 4 and 6 P.M. If you don't have an appointment one night, call until 8 P.M.
5. Ask for the appointment. Don't call to make conversation. Ask for the appointment.
6. Don't rely on telemarketing alone. Use several of the other lead generators at the same time.

In-House Telemarketing Specialists

In-house telemarketing involves hiring full-time staff to make telemarketing calls for the sales department. Or a telemarketer can be matched with a salesperson, in which case the telemarketer makes appointments for only one salesperson. The difference between this method and the personal calling method is the number of hours worked and the number of calls made.

In-house telemarketers usually work four to eight hours a day, five to six days a week. Telemarketers can make calls to business locations during the day and make residential calls later in the afternoon. The recommended hours for a full eight-hour schedule are 12 to 8 P.M.

There are advantages and disadvantages with in-house telemarketing.

Advantages

1. It is easier to hire qualified salespeople when you have leads to distribute.
2. It is easier to train new salespeople. Trainees can go on appointments with senior salespeople when you're sure the senior salespeople will have appointments.
3. It is easier to manage the efforts of salespeople.
4. It is easier to evaluate sales ability when they have frequent opportunities to sell. You control your volume. You decide how much business you want to do, and you hire accordingly.

Disadvantages

1. In-house lead generation programs, done well, are expensive and require considerable start-up capital.
2. The quality of the appointment is often less than that of an appointment set by a salesperson. Professional telemarketers argue this point, but my experience says it's so.
3. Telemarketers are usually paid by the hour and by the lead set. They also receive a bonus when the sale is made. The

lead bonus often becomes telemarketers' focus, causing them to "hard close" the appointment. The result can be a "no-show." In other words, no one is home when the salesperson arrives, or only one member of a couple is there (a "one-legged" appointment). In either case, the lead is not good. Good telemarketing operations measure competence according to appointments set as well as appointment-to-sit ratio, in other words, the number of good appointments in relation to the number of bad appointments.

Because a percentage of appointments are bad, salespeople can develop a bad attitude about telemarketed leads. They choose not to keep the appointment, try to verify the appointment before going (which is an absolute taboo), or arrive with less than a positive attitude and bungle the sale. Management needs to manage this attitude closely.

Contract Telemarketing Agencies

Contract telemarketing agencies are very much like in-house departments with the exception that you only pay for the lead or for the contract hours used on your behalf. Purchased leads from contract agencies cost twenty-five dollars per lead and more. Hourly charges are fifteen dollars per hour and more in addition to lead and sales bonuses.

Although the advantages are basically the same as those of in-house telemarketing, there are more disadvantages. First, the per lead cost is usually higher, and control becomes a factor. I have never seen this type of arrangement work well and thus would not recommend it. I don't list computer telemarketing machines into which load phone numbers because they have been shown to be ineffective. I don't recommend their use.

Before starting a telemarketing program, start with an overall plan. Decide on what you're going to do and how you will do it. You must know specifically what you intend to accomplish and then constantly measure the results. Know what your costs are going to be and don't give up on your plan too early. Telemarketing takes time and money to be successful.

The Telemarketing Plan

- Establish what you're going to do.
- Identify the markets you will target.
- Decide how you're going to implement the plan.

If you decide to go forward, do the following:

1. Establish a budget. Your lead to sale cost can run from as low as $25 per sale to as high as $750 per sale. You want to keep your costs as low as possible. Telemarketed leads should cost $250 or less per sale. That cost should be factored into your sales price. So if you pay $250 or less for a lead and you make a sale, your cost is zero. If you see your cost rising above $250, it is time to evaluate your pricing, your telemarketing manager, your telemarketers, the script being used, the closing percentage, the phone lists you are using, your salespeople, and, in short, anything that is causing your lead cost to be so high.
2. Develop telemarketing scripts.
3. Decide what type of people you wish to hire.
4. Decide where you'll find these people.
5. Plan to train staff when you find them.
6. Track telemarketers' efforts constantly. Weed out the bad and reward the good.
7. Set and monitor quality goals for your telemarketers.
8. Monitor the sales department's use of leads.
9. Interface telemarketing and sales departments. Telemarketers are salespeople.
10. Consider teaming a telemarketer with one or more salespeople. The team concept works well.

DIRECT MAIL PROGRAMS

Do you want some good advice? Don't try telemarketing without first softening prospects with a good direct mail campaign. Statistics show that prospects are more accepting of a phone call after first receiving two or three pieces of mail from your company. The mail develops name recognition. When prospects know who you are, they are more willing to talk to you.

According to national statistics, direct mail as a lead generator produces a 0.5 percent rate of return. If you send one thousand pieces of mail with a return reply card, you can expect to receive fifty replies or fewer. You can improve your return ratio by doing the following:

1. Send three pieces to the same address over a 30 to 45 day period.
2. Include a postage paid reply card as part of the mailer. People procrastinate. If you make it easy to reply, they just might.
3. Use the first few lines of the mailer and a postscript (P.S.) to get prospects' attention. It's been proved that people read P.S.'s, so make it interesting and your return rate will improve.
4. Aim your mail. Be specific with your mail programs. Shot mailing is expensive and ineffective. Decide who your best prospects are and mail to them directly.
5. Whenever possible, hand write the envelope. Wedding invitation size envelopes with a handwritten address have the greatest chance of being opened.
6. Hand stamp each envelope when possible. These envelopes are likely to be opened.

Each one of these steps increases the odds that your direct mail piece will be read. Prospects won't respond if they don't read or, worse yet, don't open the mail.

The final and most important piece of advice I can give you regarding direct mail is this: Don't send one piece of mail unless you intend to follow up with a phone call within three to five days. Direct mail followed by a phone call in three days can produce more than ten appointments for each one hundred pieces sent. This is a far cry better than 0.5 percent without the call. Why is this so you ask? Because people are procrastinators. We often see something and say to ourselves "I should look into that." However, something more important comes up and we forget or defer calling or mailing back the card. Over a short period of time the reply card either is lost or we just don't think about it again. When you call a prospect, it's much easier for them to react and take action. Procrastination has been defeated.

Direct Mail and New Salespeople

One of the best ways to get new salespeople going is to teach them and enforce a regimen of mailing twenty-five pieces of mail each day. Three days later they call twenty-five people who have already received mail. Salespeople who follow this regimen have an abundance of leads to whom to present their product. They have numerous opportunities to earn top commissions.

Direct Mail as an Advertising Vehicle

Direct mail serves as an excellent advertisement and name recognition builder. When prospects see your name over and over again they begin to see you as a solid business. They begin to equate your company name with the product or service you sell.

To whom should you mail?

- All your customers
- The people on your customers' emergency notification lists
- Previous prospects who haven't yet bought
- Parent Teacher Association membership
- Neighborhood crime watch member list
- Kiwanis, Rotary, and similar organizations
- Burglary victims
- Neighbors of burglary victims
- New homeowner lists
- New businesses
- Professionals, such as doctors, lawyers, and engineers

REFERRALS

If you ask one hundred salespeople where the bulk of their leads originate, they will tell you as much as sixty percent of their leads come from referrals.

What is a referral? A referral is a lead given to you by an existing customer. Your customers call you or you call them, they give you the names and phone numbers of friends or acquaintances they feel are prospects for your product. Sometimes the new prospects contact you and inform you that they are calling on the recommendation of your existing customer. Either way, this is a referral.

How do we get referrals? Do we assume if we do a great job for a customer they eventually will call us to give us referrals? You could, if you have lots of money in your savings account to live on in the meantime.

When do we ask for referrals? Every time you speak with your customer. The best time to ask for referrals is at the time of the sale. If the prospects had enough confidence in you and your company to spend their money, then why shouldn't they feel comfortable referring you to others. They trust you, and they believe in you. Unless they believe they are the only people on earth who are potential crime victims, they should know several people who would benefit from your product and services. Have the courage to ask for and you will most definitely receive leads.

An excellent way to ask for leads at the point of sale is as follows: After the purchase agreement has been signed, get out the emergency notification form and ask the new customers to get their address book. Explain that they will need it because you'll need several names, addresses, and phone numbers to complete the emergency notification form. When they have their address book, ask for the names, addresses, and phone numbers of the ten people they want to notify.

I know what you're thinking. You never ask for ten names on that form, and you never ask for addresses. Think of it this way: Is there a chance that when the central station has to contact people for your client in the event of an emergency that among the usual three called, no one is home? It's happened in my central station numerous times.

Do some of the emergency contacts change their phone numbers or move without notifying the central station? Sure they do, and then what's happened? There is no one to contact in case of emergency. Often the names on the list are friends or relatives. It can happen that your customer and friends go somewhere together. Then who's available in the event of a burglary or emergency? No one.

These are all good reasons to ask for ten or more names. After getting all the names, phone numbers and most important, addresses, ask the customer the following questions. Be sure to ask them exactly this way:

> Whom do you know who would benefit from learning how an ABC system could protect them from a fire or crime? Who is the first person that comes to mind who would benefit from the protection of an ABC system?

Assume the customer knows someone who would be a prospect; of course, they do. A key part of the question asked is, "Whom do you know?" rather than, "Do you know?" *Whom do you know* assumes customers know someone who would benefit from the system. Why shouldn't they know someone? The customers' isn't the only family vulnerable because of fire and crime. If you have the customers' phone directory in hand, it's easy for them to find the phone numbers to give you. Do you see how that works?

Second, what do you think you should do about the ten names on the emergency list? Aren't they all prospects, too? They sure are. With the list in hand, tell your customer you will call each of the emergency contacts to explain what to do and especially what not to do in the event they are called to respond to an emergency at the alarm location. You also will make an appointment with the contacts to explain the system installed so that in the event the contacts must go to the protected home in an emergency, they will know what the system looks like and what to do. That makes sense, doesn't it?

How do you think you're going to explain the system? You bet! You're going to do a complete demonstration of the system and its benefits. Is it possible the emergency contacts could find themselves interested in protecting themselves with an ABC system? Absolutely! Anytime anyone does something different, remodels, installs insulated windows, or buys a new car, others in the neighborhood believe they should consider doing the same. This feeling wears off, so you must strike while the iron is hot.

BIRD DOGS

Bird dogs hunt birds. Bird dogs in sales hunt leads. A bird dog is anyone who is in a position to flush leads for you. Here's a list of potential bird dogs.

> Insurance people
> Police officers
> Fire fighters
> Locksmiths
> Glaziers
> Neighborhood watch leaders
> Other salespeople
> Doctors
> Lawyers
> Bankers
> Real estate agents

Bird dogs provide leads to you for various reasons. The most common, however, is money. The average bird-dog fee I paid was $75.00. There are other reasons some of these people would steer prospects your way. For example, casualty insurance companies have a reason to help a reliable alarm company. Insurance underwriters pay agencies a bonus that is based on their loss ratio. In other words, underwriters reward agencies if the insured do not make a claim. When an insurance customer purchases a quality alarm system, the risk for burglary and fire loss decreases and the potential for a bonus to the insurance agency increases. Thus alarm systems can be good for insurance agents. However, agents expect a token of your gratitude for providing customers to you, that is, cash.

Who are the first people to find out about a burglary? The police? Yes. A glass company? Possibly. If the burglar broke a window to gain entry, the victim calls a glass company. The glazier therefore is a potential bird dog. Get together and make a deal. How about a locksmith? Often keys are stolen in a burglary, or the victim wants to change locks anyway.

Who is the first to know when someone purchases a house? The real estate salesperson is an excellent source of leads. House buyers often rely on the real estate agent to provide information about flooring, drapes, lawn care professionals, exterminators and many other services. Why shouldn't they steer people toward a reliable alarm system?

Keep your eyes open for potential bird dogs and don't be greedy. They'll make lots of money for you over the years.

COLD CALLING

Brrr! It's a chilling thought. I don't even like the name *cold calling*. Let's call it *farming*. There is no question, to be successful in the long term, you must include farming in your overall plan. It's simple and fun.

Make a list of prospects for your product and where they can be found. Then go visit them. However, let me give you one important piece of advice. Don't expect prospects to be waiting with open arms. Don't expect them to want to see you. In fact, it's best to make the call expecting that they don't want to see you at all and that they will tell you they are not interested. That way you won't be crushed when they say they're not interested. However, make sure you call on them again, and again, and again. By the third time, they'll smile when they see you. By the fourth time they'll look forward to seeing your smiling face. When they begin to like you, they start to trust you. Once they trust you, they'll buy from you.

One last thing about cold calling. *Call on prospects even if they already have what you're selling.* Who knows when they'll become dissatisfied with their current product. Who knows when they'll be opening another location and thus need your product. Persistence will pay premiums.

BUSINESS CARDS

Business cards are the least expensive form of advertising one can use. At seminars I've conducted, company owners have told me they wait thirty days or so before buying business cards for a new sales consultant. They do this to avoid "wasting money" on cards in the event the salesperson doesn't work out. How much are business cards? Fifteen to twenty-five dollars per thousand. This is a minimal expense compared with all other expenses in developing a salesperson.

Salespeople should be well stocked with business cards before completing the initial in-house training, even if you purchase instantly printed cards for an interim period. A salesperson without cards is half naked.

Every time you meet anyone, hand them your card. Anytime you send anything to anybody, include a business card. Why not? It's an inexpensive way to remind someone about what you sell.

When you begin a new career in the sales field, you should notify everyone you know about what you sell. One of the worst things that can happen to a salesperson is to go to a party, picnic, family reunion, or out for the evening and run into an acquaintance who asks, "What are you doing these days?" The salesperson says, "I'm in the security alarm business. We install, monitor, and service high-quality alarm systems." The acquaintance says, "No kidding! What a shame. I bought an alarm system just last month. Had I known you were in that business I'd have bought it from you." Talk about a crushing blow! If you don't let everyone know what you do, this is going to happen.

Buy business cards. Give them to everyone.

HOME SHOWS

I've displayed at great home shows and I've displayed at terrible shows. However, even the worst provide some leads. What follows are some features that make a show good.

1. The show charges an entry fee, which usually draws more-qualified shoppers.
2. The show is held in a convention center.
3. The promoter has advertised. Research promoters' advertising plans.
4. A good track record. In New Orleans there were at least two convention center shows. The older one, presented by the Home Builder's Association and Cahners exposition company, was always better and more profitable than the other, regardless of the time of year or location.

One of the keys to a successful appearance a home show is to remember why you're there. Your mission is to develop name recognition and, most important, pick up leads for sales appointments. Do not fall into the trap of doing complete demonstrations of your product at the show. Demonstrate enough to whet prospects' appetites, then ask for an appointment.

Displaying in well-organized and managed home shows is an excellent way to start new salespeople. In a matter of four days, (the average length of time the shows run) working two to four, four-hour shifts, a salesperson has an opportunity to talk to hundreds of potential prospects. An aggressive salesperson will make more than fifteen solid appointments. A one out of three closer will sell at five of those appointments.

Let me make one last point about home shows and how to work them. Every time I displayed at a show, I walked around before the opening checking out my competition. During the show, while on break or before going on shift, I walked around to see how my competitors were doing. Too often I saw their sales representatives sitting in the back of the booth reading a book or shooting the bull with another salesperson. When they saw someone passing in front of the booth, they glanced up with "I hope you're not planning to stop in this booth" looks on their faces. Most often the potential prospects continued walking past the booth on their way to the next booth.

If I'm going to spend the money and time to display at a home show, I'm going to get the most out of it. I'm not there to read a book or shoot the bull. My goal is to make appointments that will result in sales and commissions.

When working your shift, stand at the outer edge of the booth, look at every person walking past, smile, and say, "Are you folks considering the protection of your home with an electronic burglar and fire alarm system?"

I've had people walk up to my booth and look straight in, presumably looking at what we sell. When I looked them in the eye, smiled, and asked, "Are you folks considering the protection of your home with a burglar and fire alarm system?" they would look at me with bewildered looks on their faces and say, "Oh, yes, is that what you sell?"

Most visitors to home shows walk down aisle after aisle, past booth after booth. Sometimes they look but do not see. They glance at your booth but aren't focused on your display. They're in mental outer space. If I had been reading a book or sitting around waiting for the customer to come to me, I would have missed a prospect.

NEIGHBORHOOD ASSOCIATIONS

Neighborhood associations, parents clubs, Kiwanis, and Rotary all have one thing in common. They need speakers to address the group each month. They all have a somewhat frazzled member (especially toward the end of his term) who is responsible for finding interesting speakers for the monthly meeting. What a horrible job! After the first two or three months, this job becomes a nightmare. The club wants someone who is interesting, who can speak for twenty or thirty minutes on a subject that will be interesting to the membership. Without a speaker, the meetings become boring, and the membership stops attending meetings.

When they don't go to meetings, they wonder why they're paying dues and leave the club. As you can see, it can be an enormous responsibility to hold the title Program Chair.

Fire and crime are popular topics. You must be careful, however, not to try to sell alarm systems at the meeting. Like the home show, this isn't the place to sell. If you approach neighborhood meetings with the attitude that you're there to educate people about the twin perils of fire and crime, your image and reputation will be enhanced in the community. While you're giving a fifteen-minute talk, pass around a legal pad that asks for the name, address, and phone number of anyone who wants a free home security and fire analysis. The more interesting your talk, the more informative and eye opening it is, the better results you will see. This is definitely an area in which practice makes perfect.

If you follow the rules and do not attempt to sell to people at the meeting, and if your talk was well received, ask the program chair for a letter from the association saying so. Also ask permission to have other program chairs call her for references. In short order you will be an in-demand speaker. More important, you'll be developing a "Doctor of Security" image and leads will flow.

CUSTOMER VISITS

Regular visits to existing customers is an excellent source of leads for in-home selling. People rarely if ever receive a free home visit from an employee of a company from whom they purchased something. Think about it for a moment. Has a representative from Sears ever visited your home just to see if you're happy with the appliances you purchased from them? Not recently you say! It almost never happens.

Try this sometime. Send a letter on company stationary to fifteen customers. In your letter notify them that Jim Jones from ABC (your company) will be in their area to perform a customer service visit. Jim will be calling to arrange for a convenient appointment. Jim should wait three days and begin calling each customer, setting three daytime appointments a day. When Jim arrives he should do the following:

1. Ask the customers if they are happy with the system.
2. Ask if there is anything they would have done differently now that they've had the system for X number of years. Anything they say may lead to a sale of add-on features.
3. Ask the customers who they know who could benefit from your product.
4. Explain your company's maintenance policy program.
5. Re-sign monitoring agreements and update emergency notification information.
6. Conduct a courtesy check of the system battery and of infrequently used sensors, such as those on a door or window that is rarely opened.

This program, if worked diligently, will produce leads and add-on sales and is an excellent way to start new salespeople.

TIP CLUBS

Tip clubs are organizations that meet usually weekly, most often for an early breakfast or coffee. Basic rules of such clubs are that only one member from each type of business can belong and that all members bring in a lead to share with the group each week. A tip club that would benefit an alarm salesperson would include an architect, builder, insurance agent, plumber, electrician, carpet installer, and a decorator. Each of these people sell their services to identical clients. If someone is building a home and hires the member architect, she would provide the client's name at the next meeting. As a result, each of the other members know before their competitors the name, address, and phone number of a prospect.

The only problem I've ever encountered with tip clubs is finding one to join. Rarely does a member resign. You have to wait for some one to die or resign—unless you start your own club. If it's difficult for you to join a club because it allows only one member from each type company, you can believe architects, builders, insurance agents, and others are having the same problem. Research your community. Find out with whom you'd like to form a team, then ask them if they're in a club. If their answer is no, sign them up.

CRIME PREVENTION OFFICERS

Every large police department and most small departments have one or more crime prevention officers. Their job is to meet with neighborhood groups and individuals to lecture or make recommendations on how citizens can protect themselves against crime. As usual, crime prevention departments are understaffed and underfunded. They can use help. Don't expect them to be waiting for you to show up. As in any other cold call, expect a less than friendly greeting the first time you call. However, persistence pays premiums. Call back again and again. Offer to help with meetings. Offer to provide generic literature addressing the crime problem that officers can distribute at meetings. They'll accept the offer and over a period of time suggest you put your name on the literature you give them. If you develop a good reputation with these officers, they may offer to allow you to conduct a portion of each meeting. When they do that, they are recommending you.

One final note on crime prevention departments: departments in small cities are often easier to approach and more open to your help. Seek them out, go to their meetings, introduce yourself, and then offer your help. If the help you give is of a generic nature, officers will want to take advantage of the help you're offering.

RADIO, TELEVISION, NEWSPAPER

Television and radio are expensive methods to generate leads. Unless you have deep pockets and lots of money to invest, don't use radio and television. On the other hand, radio and television can be the fastest way to develop name recognition. You won't be overwhelmed by calls for sales, but your name will begin to be recognized. Newspaper advertising is less expensive than radio or television advertising, but it also is not cost effective.

Radio, television, and newspaper advertising for the alarm sales industry has not been cost effective for several reasons. The most prevalent reasons are as follows:

1. The psychological law of self exception causes many people to believe they don't have a problem. If they believe they don't have a problem, why pay attention to the radio or television advertisement?
2. Unless you have a large advertising budget, the advertising doesn't make an impact. Advertising works best when aimed and repeated regularly. Repetition pays.

BILLBOARDS, COUPONS, SCHOOL AND CHURCH BULLETINS

Coupons

Don't waste your money. Coupons work if you sell hamburgers, dry cleaning, film developing, or haircuts. Your advertisement to sell alarm systems will get lost in the package of other coupons, and the psychological law of self exception still applies.

Billboards

If you're interested in developing name recognition and any leads advertising can produce, billboard advertising is the best I've found. To be effective, billboard locations and quantities are important. On what streets or highways does your type of prospect travel? That's where the boards should be.

Keep your message on the billboard brief and to the point. Busy boards are difficult to read. For the same reason, phone numbers should not be used unless your number can be converted to an easily recognized and remembered word, for example, 555-SAFE.

School and Church Bulletins

If you consider the advertisement a donation, place it. I believe in supporting the church I attend and the schools my children attend. As an advertising lead generator, it is not useful.

YOUR COMPANY VEHICLES

Your company van or truck can often serve as a top-ten lead and name recognition generator. Five vehicles crossing a city eight hours a day, five to six days a week, have the visual impact of twenty or more cars. In other words, consumers who see your vehicles think to themselves, "ABC company must have twenty company cars. I see them everywhere." For this reason, your vehicle should look as good as you can make it look.

An alarm company in the Orlando area, Alarm Detection Systems, uses their vehicles to the maximum. Company vans are distinctly marked and are painted yellow with red lettering. One can identify one of their vehicles from almost any distance. When you are following one of their trucks, you can't help but read the message:

YOU ARE FOLLOWING A BURGLAR

alarm company vehicle
555-1000

To carry the advertising further, the company's building, which is on a busy street, also is painted yellow with red lettering, and the business cards are yellow and red.

Dick Huffer, the president of Alarm Detection Systems, told me at a seminar that he can recall several instances in which prospects called in as a result of seeing his vividly marked van. What Alarm Detection has is a fleet of rolling billboards.

If your business often takes you into a business district in which the buildings are two stories or taller, and if you don't have ladders on the top of your truck, spend a little extra and paint your company name and phone number on the top of the truck or van. Think about it. People in a downtown area look out windows and what they see are the tops of cars and trucks. This gives you another opportunity to get your name in front of potential prospects.

YARD SIGNS

Yard signs are miniature billboards. Yard signs that are easily recognizable tell prospects that other people are protected by ABC company. There is a degree of comfort knowing that I am not the only person who is making the decision to purchase from that company. When prospects drive down the street and see lots of ABC signs, they are inclined to call ABC. All those people who bought from ABC can't be wrong.

Yard signs sell systems and are inexpensive. A key requirement for an effective yard sign is that it be easily recognizable to potential prospects walking or driving down a street. An elaborate, cleverly designed logo may look good on a letterhead but not on a yard sign. The sign is not there to impress you or your competitors. It's there to inform a potential prospect. When designing your sign, be sure the name of your company can be read and understood from as far away as possible.

FLYERS, DOOR HANGERS

There are two ways to distribute door hangers and flyers. One way is to contract with a company who does it for you or hire your own employee. The other way is to have your salespeople distribute them.

Flyers

Flyers, as is direct mail, are only as effective as the telephone follow-up conducted after the flyers are distributed. Also as with direct mail, areas should be targeted for maximum effect. If you hand out door hangers or flyers in the same neighborhoods on two or three occasions, you will find that your success ratio increases.

Hang flyers in areas where burglaries have occurred immediately after the burglary. Remember, your flyers should be designed to evoke interest in making an appointment. They should not be designed to attempt to sell your product.

"Pardon Our Noise" Door Hangers

Every time you make a sale, hang a door hanger on eight houses or more on each side of the new customer and on sixteen houses across the street. This can be accomplished in less than an hour, slightly longer if someone is at home at one of the houses. The door hanger begins with an apology for any inconvenience caused by the noise from the siren while your crews are testing the new security alarm system you are installing at the Jones's home. It goes on to say that the Joneses have taken the step necessary to protect their family from the twin perils of fire and crime by installing a quality ABC security alarm system. It closes by offering to demonstrate the system the Jones family purchased. A follow-up phone call should be made within two days of the door hanging.

PASS-CARD LISTS

Every time you sell a system, ask for a minimum of ten emergency notification names, addresses, and phone numbers. I'm aware you usually ask for only three. However, ten is best for you and your customer. Why? Isn't it possible that with only three names, none of the three will be home when an emergency occurs? It happens all the time. Are the odds better with ten names? Of course.

Every name on the emergency list is a prospect, or at the very least, a potential prospect. Send each one a letter and then follow the letter with a phone call. Make an appointment to explain to the emergency contact what should be done and, just as important, what should not done in the event they're called to respond to the Jones's alarm system. Show the emergency contact what the Jones family installed to protect themselves and then offer to perform a free security survey for the emergency contact.

THOSE YOU KNOW

Whom do you know? Send an announcement card to every person you know to inform them you are in the alarm business. Who knows when someone will need protection. If they don't know you're in the business of providing alarm systems, or whatever product you sell, they won't call you. Conversely, they'll go out of their way to help you by calling to inform you of a sales opportunity. From time to time, send reminder cards.

ACCOUNTS PAYABLE LIST

Who pays the bills in your home? Every time you send a payment to anyone, include your business card in the envelope—even to the power company and mortgage company. Who opens the mail at the power company? A secretary? An accounting clerk? Do they live in houses? Do they know people who live in houses? After these people receive a dozen or more cards from you and a friend of theirs finds themselves needing an alarm system, do you think they'll know who sells alarm systems? Business cards are expensive, mail them out. What do you have to lose?

REPOSSESSED HOUSE RENTAL PROGRAM

Traveling the country conducting seminars, I have the opportunity of sharing selling tips with thousands of salespeople. At one of those seminars, a salesperson explained a program he had developed. Because so many homes are repossessed every day, banks, savings and loan institutions, and mortgage companies are finding themselves with an everincreasing inventory of houses they are trying to sell. Some sit on their inventory for several months.

Empty houses are targets for burglars and vandals. The salesperson I met developed a rental program designed especially for repossessed houses. He rents a basic wireless system to the lender for a daily rate of five dollars for a minimum of thirty days. Because the houses aren't moving fast, the income stream is quite lucrative.

YELLOW PAGES ADVERTISING

It is necessary to be in the yellow pages if for no other reason than to give a customer who is looking for your number an easy way of finding it. Other than that, I'm not a big fan of the yellow pages. Unless you are selling low-end systems, yellow pages callers are usually price shoppers. You will sell to a few of the shoppers, but you should constantly measure your results in relation to the return on your investment.

Several years ago, I was talked into signing up with a national advertising agency who would handle any and all advertising we needed. The yellow pages was one of the services. The incentive for my company was discounted rates, so we signed up. To sign up, we were required to send a letter to the local yellow pages company informing them that all advertising for our company from that day forward would be placed by the national service. As luck would have it, the national company failed to place our yellow pages advertisement that year. In April, when the new book hit the streets, we discovered the oversight. We knew we were doomed. We were sure our business would suffer greatly. Not so! Much to our surprise, we saw no appreciable loss in sales. When we considered the money we saved by not paying for the yellow pages advertising, we made profit on the mistake.

USED DEMO KITS

Another alarm salesperson I met found a productive use for outdated demonstration kits. If you've been in the business more than ten years and use demonstration kits, you are now the owner of one or more outdated kits. Rather than using his as a door stop or having it take up space in the stock room, this salesperson found a good use for it. He donates the kits to the local police department to be lent to rape victims until they can make other arrangements or until they feel safe.

Rape victims often are frightened being alone for the first week or two after the rape. They're afraid of every noise they hear and look to the police for comfort. Police don't have the personnel to station a unit outside a victim's home, nor do they have the time to patrol enough to give the victim the security she needs. The donated alarm is programmed to the alarm company's central monitoring station and is identified with a number only. When the police place the unit in a victim's home, they notify the central station that unit number XX is installed. For reasons of privacy, the alarm company doesn't know where the alarm is, they only know the number. Of course, the police know where they placed it and are able to provide fast response.

The police are happy with the arrangement because it allows them to help the victim without placing an impossible burden on staffing requirements. The victim receives the peace of mind afforded by the panic button in the demonstration equipment and by the knowledge that help is only the push of a button away. The alarm company is happy because it is able to help victims and the police and has developed a relationship with the police that in the long run can prove profitable. Because the alarm company's name is on the demonstration equipment, there is a better than even chance that if the victim decides to purchase an alarm system she will call the company whose alarm provided her with peace of mind at a time of great need. This is definitely a win-win-win situation.

CONCLUSION

Whoever said selling is easy? It's not easy. If it were, everyone would succeed in sales and we would have a worldwide glut of trained professional salespeople, and the potential for high incomes would drop. It would be another case of supply and demand. Incomes are up in the sales arena because good, trained salespeople are difficult to find. Ask any company who employs salespeople and they will agree.

Sales is hard work, but it's rewarding. To quote the late Norm Eisenstat, of *The Science of Selling Alarm Systems*, "Selling is the world's best-paying 'hard' job and conversely, the world's worst-paying 'easy' job." Sales doesn't require a high intellect, nor does it require years of study. It does require some study, persistence, belief in self, determination, and an unshakable desire to succeed.

If you apply the principles I have shared with you in this book; if you study each chapter over and over until you internalize its message; if you have the courage to practice, practice, and practice some more; if you train your internal computer to see yourself as a winning professional sales leader, you will succeed on purpose.

$$CI + PPA = SOP$$

Correct Image + Planned Positive Action = Success On Purpose

Good luck and great selling!

Index

AND IN THE WARM-UP STEP
SAY "ARE YOU A COLLECTOR
OF ANTIQUES" WHEREUPON
I WOULD RESPOND, THEN
THE SALESPERSON WOULD
~~RESPOND~~ ASK, "WHY DID YOU
PICK THAT PARTICULAR PERIOD
OF ANTIQUES TO COLLECT?"
THEN I WOULD PROBABLY BEGIN
TELLING YOU MY LIFE STORY.
ALL IT TAKES TO
WARM PEOPLE ARE A FEW
PROBING QUESTIONS ABOUT
A SUBJECT THEY LIKE TO
TALK ABOUT. WHEN THEY
BEGIN TELLING YOU ABOUT
WHAT THEY ENJOY, THEY
BEGIN TO RELAX, AND

WHAT IS A WARM-UP?
How IS It Done?

Everyone HAS SOMETHING
THEY ARE PROUD OF OR
SOMETHING THEY ~~ARE PROUD~~
LIKE TO TALK ABOUT. THEY
USUALLY DISPLAY WHAT THEY
LIKE TO TALK ABOUT in A
PROMINENT PLACE. SO VISITORS
CAN AND WILL SE IT.
FOR EXAMPLE, I LOVE
TO COLLECT ANTIQUES. IF
YOUR A SALEPERSON AND YOU
ARE in MY HOME MORE
THAN THREE MINUTES AND
I HAVEN'T FIGURED THAT OUT,
YOU JUST HAVEN'T BEEN
LOOKING. An OBSERVANT
SALESPERSON WOULD PICK UP

Begin to become A FRIEND.
WHEN THEY LIKE YOU, they
WANT TO TRUST you.

POLICE DEPTS.
  ASK FOR. Community.
  Laison OFFICER.

FIRE Depts · Same thing,

Large Appliance Stores
Demo Boards

Summer Plan Cold calls
early Because of Beach

Incorporate the fact that
each Rep must do _NO?_ OF
Registered leads per week.

These must be registered
with the sales manager each
day —

Sales Rep must speak to
Mg. every day —